T0182669

To:
From:
Date:

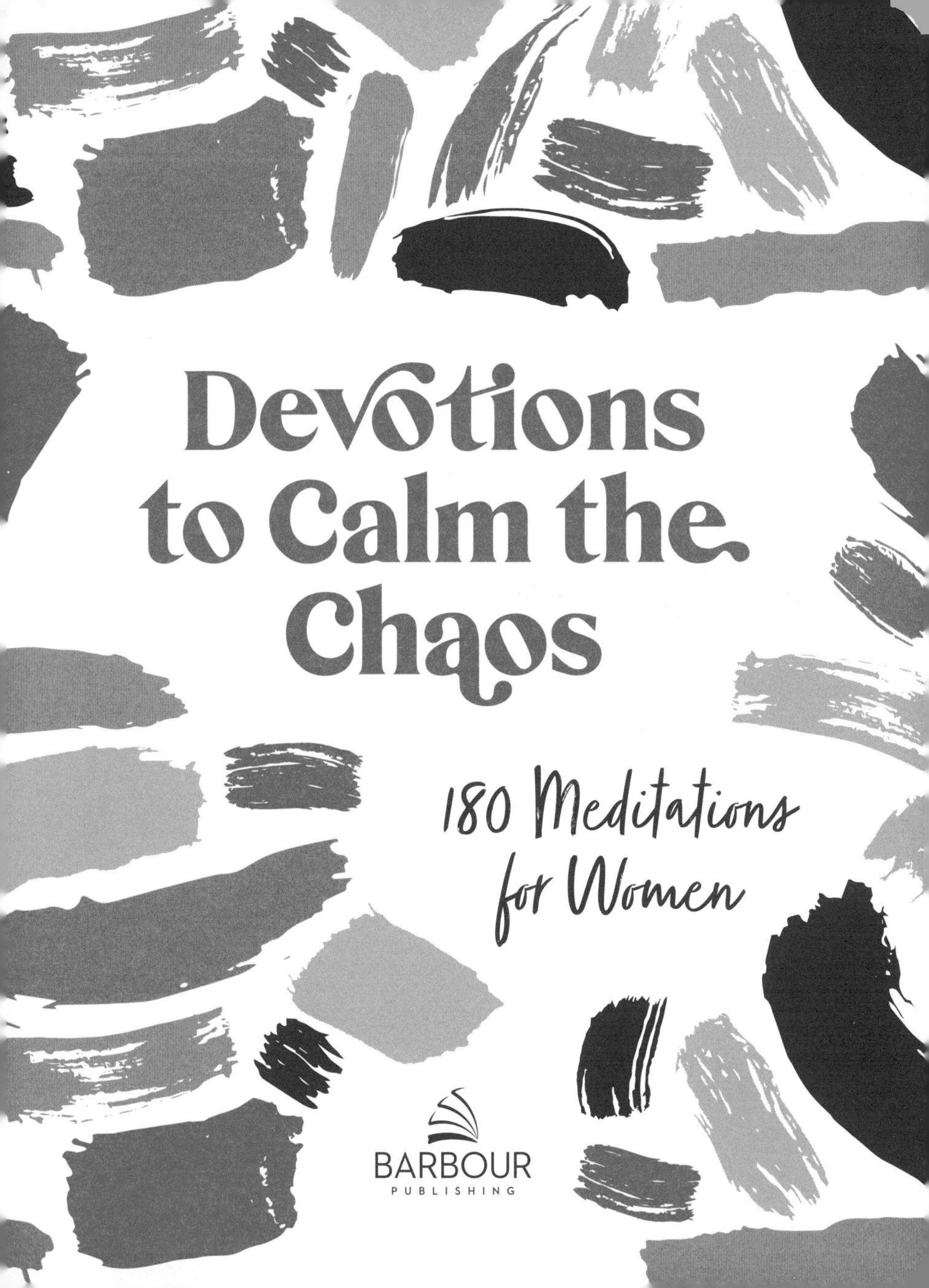

Devotions to Calm the Chaos

180 Meditations for Women

BARBOUR
PUBLISHING

Print ISBN 978-1-63609-802-9
Adobe Digital Edition (.epub) 978-1-63609-937-8

Cover Design: Greg Jackson, Thinkpen Design

Published by Barbour Publishing, Inc., 1810 Barbour Drive, Uhrichsville, Ohio 44683, www.barbourbooks.com

Our mission is to inspire the world with the life-changing message of the Bible.

Printed in China.

Introduction

Daily life is filled with all kinds of chaos—some big, some little—and *all* the pandemonium can get in the way of our walk with Jesus. These devotions can help.

This lovely collection of 180 inspiring readings will comfort and calm your soul, no matter what the day holds. With each turn of the page, you'll encounter regular reminders of the heavenly Father's faithfulness and love. And you'll come to understand and trust that He will make good on His promises to you.

As you grow in your faith, you'll be drawn to spend purposeful, spiritually refreshing time with the Master Creator, the one and only Chaos-Calmer.

Be blessed, dear one!

God, make a fresh start in me,
shape a Genesis week from the chaos of my life.
Don't throw me out with the trash,
or fail to breathe holiness in me.
Bring me back from gray exile,
put a fresh wind in my sails! . . .
I'll sing anthems to your life-giving ways.
Unbutton my lips, dear God;
I'll let loose with your praise.

Psalm 51:10–12, 14–15 msg

Like a Friend

You have turned my mourning into joyful dancing.

Psalm 30:11 NLT

A little time spent with a friend over a cup of tea can work wonders on a down day. The kindness and understanding of a friend can turn everything around, transforming a sour mood into a cheerful one.

Think of how life-changing it would be to have a cup of tea with Jesus. Imagine what a good listener He would be, how His compassion alone would alter your disposition. And because He knows you even better than you know yourself, you could trust Him with your heart's desires, your deepest fears, and your brightest joys. Like no one else, Jesus can turn your day, your week, your year into cause for rejoicing.

Tidy Up Your Heart

Let us strip off every weight that slows us down.

HEBREWS 12:1 NLT

Yesterday's dirty dishes are calling. The laundry pile has grown into a mountain. Dust coats the coffee table like a thin blanket. If only you could make it all disappear, you could start fresh. Removing clutter feels good, making time and energy for all the things you want to do.

You can experience a similar result when you clean up your spiritual life. The burdening clutter of negative thinking and bad choices keeps you from accomplishing what you are called to do. But God gives you the grace and ample opportunities to clean up your act. Gather up the disarray of your life, hold it out before God, and allow Him to remove the burden from you. When spiritual clutter starts piling up again, remember—you can repeat the process every day if you need to.

Change of Season

To everything there is a season,
a time for every purpose under heaven.
ECCLESIASTES 3:1 NKJV

We've likely all had times in our lives when everything seemed to fall into place. We cherish the memories of those times and long to repeat them, but like the calendar year, our lives are made up of seasons. Soon enough, we enter a season when nothing seems to go right. That's not the case, of course, but when we dwell on the negative we wonder if we'll ever feel good about ourselves again. Our dreams seem far away.

The thing about seasons is that they come and go. With each change in your life you're given a fresh opportunity to recapture the hope you once had. God placed your hopes and dreams in you, and He knows you want to experience the joy of seeing them fulfilled. You only need to open your heart, step out in faith, and trust Him when He makes it clear that it's time to enter that season of fulfillment.

Timeless

"Can all your worries add a single moment to your life?"
MATTHEW 6:27 NLT

Wouldn't it be wonderful if we could add an occasional hour to a day? The ticking clock is an ominous sound when we have so much to do and our day is slipping away. Our perceived lack of time robs us of joy and much needed leisure.

What is time to God? It's neither an annoyance nor a benefit. So why are we so burdened by it? Our freedom in Christ can release us from enslavement to the tyranny of time; we need to learn to accomplish what God wants us to—that and no more. And then, we need to rest in His peace.

God wants you to relinquish your hold on time—or rather, the hold time has on you. Lay down your ever-growing to-do lists, commit your time to Him, and relax in His presence, knowing that He has given you all the time you need to do what is truly essential.

As a Child

"Anyone who will not receive the kingdom of God like a little child will never enter it."

LUKE 18:17 NIV

Watching children play can be so comforting. The carefree imagination of a young child is open to so many possibilities; life is filled with spontaneous adventures. Watching them can make us long for that kind of freedom again, the freedom to change course and play with building blocks when we no longer feel like coloring.

Our challenge as adults is to approach Jesus with all the spontaneity and adventurous spirit of a little child. With a sense of wonder and expectancy, we can find the freedom we long for in His presence. With a mind unburdened by duty and obligation, we can actually hear the words of healing and restoration that He speaks to us. Go to Him as His child, unafraid, trusting Him to hold you in His arms. Tell Him your deepest secrets and relish His fatherly love. It's in His presence that you can be sure to find respite from your adult worries.

Blessed Scars

You died to this life, and your real life
is hidden with Christ in God.
COLOSSIANS 3:3 NLT

The view from the window was especially lovely early in the morning. Fog floated in and out of the valleys, hiding all but the tops of the trees. The sun reached to shine past the clouds, spreading its rays on the hillsides. The shadows made the scars in the landscape come to life. Each crevasse and rock had its special place in the overall landscape.

You may wish you could hide the scars in the picture of your life. But those impressions have meaning and purpose; everything you see as a scar is evidence of a wound that God has healed. God has taken those crevasses and piles of rocks and turned them into a beautiful portrait of who you are. When you look at yourself, you may see only the blemishes. But God, and those who care to look closely, see the beauty in your uniqueness.

Under Pressure

We know that in all things God works for the good of those who love him.

Romans 8:28 niv

Mother always said that her apple pies weren't good unless they boiled over in the oven. Somehow that signaled to her that they had cooked just right. She didn't mind cleaning up the mess, as long as everyone else praised her pies.

Sometimes our emotions spill over when we're in the heat of things. We think we have our emotions under control. But as the situation gets hotter and hotter, our simmer turns into a boil. We lose control, boil over, and leave a mess behind.

We hardly make a good impression when that happens; we can't expect anyone to praise us when we boil over. God knows when we're at our boiling point, and He is there to help us control our emotions. But remember this: Even when we do boil over, He helps us clean up the mess. He is quick to forgive and restore. There is simply no mess too big for Him.

In His Strength

Be strong in the Lord and in his mighty power.

Ephesians 6:10 niv

Leaves dance along the pavement, moving as if they had a life of their own. Likewise, the arms of a windmill spin as if their movement is self-propelled. We know, however, that it's the invisible power of the wind that provides the energy needed to set both the leaves and the windmill in motion.

We also know that it is God who breathes His power to help us move along the path He has chosen for us. Like the wind, He is invisible, yet we see the evidence of His impact on our lives. At times, we may wonder if He is still working on our behalf. But then we sense that gentle nudge—or that strong gale—and we have all the evidence we need of His presence once again.

God is the wind, the invisible force, that lifts us above our circumstances and enables us to dance amid our difficulties. And He is the power and the energy that gives us the strength to keep ourselves in motion spiritually, despite the opposing forces that tempt us to quit.

He's Always There

"Yet I am not alone, for my Father is with me."
John 16:32 NIV

Have you ever felt as if everyone in your life has scattered, leaving you alone and lonely? In today's busy world, there are times when cultivating intimacy with friends or even maintaining family relationships is more difficult than it should be.

Women especially feel the emptiness of scattered families. Our loved ones leave a hole in our heart when they move away, leave no time for us in their overscheduled lives, or close themselves off from us for whatever reason. We long for the patchwork of our tribe to be closely knit together.

At all times, however, our heavenly Father fills the void left by our loved ones. He is constantly by our side, comforting us and providing the intimacy we need. He is there to mend our broken heart, give us new purpose, and fulfill our desire for relationship. He understands our loneliness—and gently calls us to recognize His faithful, loving, and compassionate presence.

We Need the Rain

The Lord is good, a strong refuge when trouble comes.

Nahum 1:7 NLT

The brightness of the summer sky and the sun's warmth cheer us up after the gloomy skies of winter. It's a scientific fact that sunlight increases the chemicals in our brain that elevate our mood. But it's not possible to have sunshine every day. There are rainy days to contend with, and dark skies may keep us indoors.

When the rain falls on our life, we don't always experience it as a refreshing remedy for our parched condition. Even knowing how valuable the rain is at times is not enough to help us appreciate the storms that come our way. But we should rejoice in the rain—and even in those seemingly destructive storms. Why? Because new life springs from the soil of our soul when God showers us with His blessings. The seeds He planted in us, possibly many seasons earlier, need gentle rain for steady growth—and occasional storms to strengthen growth.

Help for Success

Commit your way to the Lord, trust also in Him.

Psalm 37:5 NKJV

Whenever we discover a passion in our lives, most of us start out with a vision and all the excitement we need to get going on a project that will fuel our enthusiasm. It feels so good in the beginning. Then time passes and the vision blurs, leaving us with a sense of drudgery instead of exhilaration. It's so easy to consider packing it in. But if the project is meant to be, it's always too early to quit.

Whether our passion is a hobby, a career-related project, a relationship goal, or a lofty dream, the glory will likely fade over time, for any number of reasons. We forget our original commitment and give up on seeing it through to the end. We haven't staked our claim deep enough.

It may be too early to quit, but it's never too late to start again. And we know where to turn for a fresh start; God can renew our vision, recharge our batteries, and prod us to revisit our dream. He is the master at restoring lost joy and passion!

Free from Pain

Surely he took up our pain and bore our suffering.
ISAIAH 53:4 NIV

Physical infirmities affect more than just the body. Whether our physical problems result from accident, disease, or aging, we find we must make mental and spiritual adjustments as well as make accommodation for our physical limitations. We can't do what once came so easily to us; the woman we see in the mirror doesn't reflect the youthfulness we feel on the inside. It's not unusual to begin to question God and pray to be released from chronic pain, illness, or degeneration.

It seems that no one can comfort us when we feel defeated by the condition we're in—no one except our Creator. He understands the pain we feel in every area of our lives. When we look to Him for relief from our suffering, we can't help but be reminded that neither this earth nor this body is our home. One day we will be transformed, renewed in every way. That's a promise we can stand on today—and run and skip and dance on tomorrow.

Love Like This

Indeed, nothing in all creation will ever be able to separate us from the love of God.
Romans 8:39 NLT

To be yoked to God is to experience an unbreakable bond of love. We seek this kind of love in the world, but it's not to be found. Only the Father has the capacity to love us perfectly, and only God has the power to prevent anyone or anything from separating us from His love. That's a staggering reality. Is it even possible to fully appreciate His kind of love?

Despite all of this, we still shut Him out at times—not because we want to be cut off from Him but because we feel we need to hide our shame. We fear He will reject us for the sin in our lives, even though we know better. In those times, we need to cling to the assuring words in the verse above and be confident in His unfailing, unconditional love. Nothing can separate us from His love—nothing.

He Is There

"Do not fear, for I am with you; do not be dismayed, for I am your God."
ISAIAH 41:10 NIV

Your young child runs out into the street, and your heart is stricken with terror. A police car stops in front of your house, and overwhelming fear makes your legs weak. In those and similar circumstances, fear is understandable; the suddenness of the situation catches you off guard, and the worst possible outcome races through your mind.

But most of us experience a kind of ongoing fear that is rooted in the uncertain and the unknown. That kind of fear doesn't disappear on its own; it grows and festers until it robs us of our joy. Only by remembering who God is—our ever-present protector—and making a conscious decision to believe that He is always near can we ever expect to let go of the fear that besieges us and embrace the protection of the Father.

He Knows Your Need

"Come to Me, all you who labor and are heavy laden, and I will give you rest."

MATTHEW 11:28 NKJV

Most women know how it feels to be worn to a frazzle. We've known days, or even seasons, when we had to keep going despite illness, weariness, or the temptation to go to bed and never get up again. We have no time to take care of ourselves the way we should; utter fatigue has become a constant companion. When do we get to rest?

Jesus knows all too well how we feel. The crush of people who surrounded Him and needed what He, and only He, had to offer was far more demanding than anything we have known. He was tested and pushed to His physical and emotional limits, but He continued to minister to the people because He knew His time on earth was short. He extends that same compassion to us today, offering to us the kind of rest that He, and only He, can provide—the kind that removes our burdens and refreshes our spirit.

The Other Side of Failure

Through the LORD*'s mercies we are not consumed,*
because His compassions fail not.
LAMENTATIONS 3:22 NKJV

Many a successful person has maintained that the road to their success was paved with failure. The same holds true for spiritual success—the maturing of our faith and our relationship with God. The wonderful reality is that after we fail, God offers a fresh start—every time. His mercy extends beyond what we deserve or could hope for.

We may grieve for a while over our failure, but eventually the time comes to pick ourselves up, hand our failure over to God, and allow Him to show us how to turn it into a stepping-stone toward greater trust in Him and therefore a deeper relationship with Him. His love and care walk us through each step in the journey toward healing and growth. As we continue to look to God, we learn that we will not be consumed by our failures. His compassion and mercy assures us of that.

Reflect God's Giving

God has given each of you a gift from his great variety of spiritual gifts.
1 Peter 4:10 NLT

With so much to do on any given day, it's easy to neglect the spiritual gifts God has given to each one of us, gifts designed to be a blessing to others. Two people who have the same gift—say, the gift of teaching or hospitality—will apply that gift in unique ways that serve the individual needs of the recipients.

If it's been awhile since you've used your gift, pull it out and dust it off. Breathe new life into it and let it shine, reflecting the love and glory of God. Your gift, and your specific way of sharing it with others, may make a much-needed difference in someone else's life—which is what God intended when He gave it to you.

The Best Instruction

I will instruct you and teach
you in the way you should go.
Psalm 32:8 niv

Another fork in the road, another decision to make. Advice comes from many directions, but none of it seems to fit. What's more, each choice includes its own set of "ifs," and we don't know which way to go. It seems there's nowhere to turn to get the answers we need to move forward. Over the course of our lives, we face such challenges many times over.

Our ultimate instructor, the Master Teacher, will always steer us in the right direction. It doesn't matter what the question is; God knows which way we should go. We need to play our part, of course, seeking His guidance, listening for it, and then following it. No more guessing, no more hesitation. Knowing that it is God who has pointed us in a certain direction can give us peace of mind and confidence in the decisions we make.

You Can Tell Him

God has surely listened and has heard my prayer.

Psalm 66:19 niv

It's such a joy to know that someone is actually listening to you, isn't it? The art of listening intently is one that doesn't come naturally to most people, and it needs to be cultivated. It seems that even our well-meaning friends or family seldom give us their full attention—nor do we give them ours. We long to be heard in the deepest sense, but deep listening is a rare commodity.

God is there to listen to our most intimate thoughts. Out of His love, the God of the universe always hears the cry of our heart, whether or not we openly express it. His Word promises that He not only listens but also answers our pleas and guides us all the way to the end of our struggle. We can be assured that our God, a God of endless love and compassion, will always give us His full attention.

Give It Away

God will generously provide all you need.
Then you will always have everything you need
and plenty left over to share with others.
2 Corinthians 9:8 NLT

How long has it been since you felt as if your needs had been met? As we evaluate our needs against our wants, most of us would have to admit that because of God's great generosity, we indeed have more than we can use. Sharing from our abundance not only brings joy to others; it also helps us to see more clearly the folly of seeking security in material possessions, much of which we don't need anyway.

When we receive of God's supply, we can then be part of His provision to someone else. There is power in giving, enough to lift us out of our self-imposed reliance on stuff. We find new pleasure in participating in God's blessing to others, and in return we are doubly blessed in ways we could not have anticipated. There are no losers in this plan—only winners.

Refreshing Union

If anyone is in Christ, he is a new creation; old things have passed away; behold, all things have become new.

2 Corinthians 5:17 NKJV

Some days it seems as if we will never again have that sense of newness that once characterized our life—especially our life with God. We know we aren't washed up yet, but somehow the vibrancy we once experienced seems gone forever. What happened to the freshness of our faith, the sense of wonder that made us feel alive? Have we just gotten old?

Jesus said that He lives in us. If He truly does, how could we ever go stale? To "become" new implies an ongoing action. We are new in Him every day of our life. The old, unproductive things drop away, leaving us with our regenerating life with Christ. When we grab hold of this truth, our eyes are opened to see what new things He has for us each day.

While We Are Here

"In this world you will have trouble.
But take heart! I have overcome the world."
John 16:33 NIV

As we listen to the disturbing news coming from around the world, we are perplexed at the severe decline of morality, integrity, and godliness. Even when events happen far away from us, they affect our sense of security and well-being. What all this says about the future of humanity is enough to make us question God and wonder why He doesn't fix everything.

Jesus has conquered all the things that cause trouble in our world. He wants us to remember that our home is not here on earth; it's in heaven. While we wait to join Him there, we have a sure and solid refuge from the devastating consequences of living in a sinful environment. God is our fortress—and we can be encouraged in knowing He has already won the battle.

Run to Him

In the day of trouble he will keep me safe in his dwelling.

PSALM 27:5 NIV

Do you remember what it felt like when you were a child and knew you could run home when you were frightened? Just as children need the safety of a parent's protection, we need a place where we can go to find shelter from the storms of life. We may arrive drenched and exhausted from the effort, but knowing there's a safe haven ahead comforts us even as the storms rage.

There are many dangers in this world, and we cannot escape them unless we are in God's safe house. Where He dwells, nothing can ever truly harm us. When we run to Him, He opens the door to us, spreading His protective arm to cover us.

Ready for You

"The Lord, He is the One who goes before you."
Deuteronomy 31:8 NKJV

When you are heading into unknown territory, it's a relief to know that someone has gone ahead of you to secure your destination. A guide, a champion, or a scout is of great value to the one who comes behind, unsure of what she might encounter.

The Lord is your guide, champion, and scout in any situation, any battle. His power and might can thwart any enemy before you ever step onto unfamiliar and potentially dangerous soil. He is way ahead of you, taking care of every detail of your journey, preparing safe havens where you can rest in His protection, and building a dwelling place for you when you reach your destination. There is no need for fear or dread. He has it all under His control—and He always has your best interests at heart.

Count on It

Because of his glory and excellence,
he has given us great and precious promises.
2 PETER 1:4 NLT

As we mature, we come to depend less and less on promises made by even the most faithful people. We've seen too many promises broken, and we have to admit that we too have at times been the promise breaker. Human frailty, unforeseen circumstances, even forgetfulness can cause people to go back on their word. To protect ourselves from disappointment, we don't put too much stock in promises.

People may let us down because of their humanity, but God isn't bound by human limitations. He is bound by His own character, which ensures us that His intentions will be manifested just as He says they will. He is free to offer unlimited promises and more than able to deliver them. His motivation is love, which is the very definition of who God is. He cannot fail, He will not disappoint, and He does what He says He will do.

You're His

Having predestined us to adoption as sons by Jesus Christ to Himself, according to the good pleasure of His will.

EPHESIANS 1:5 NKJV

For many adopted children, the thought of having been given up at birth is a painful reality. Even though they were handpicked to be included in a family, it is sometimes difficult to deal with their perceived rejection by their birth parents. No matter how loving their adoptive parents are, some adopted children still struggle with the question of identity. Who am I, really?

Like an adopted child, you have been chosen! Even before the foundation of the world was set in place, God chose you to be His child. He created you for His pleasure and brought you into His family for your blessing. Who wouldn't want to be chosen to have a relationship with the Creator of the universe? To be chosen for such a purpose is far beyond our human comprehension, and yet it is the truth about the Father's love and desire for us—and about our identity.

Everlasting Covenant

He who is joined to the Lord is one spirit with Him.
1 CORINTHIANS 6:17 NKJV

The joining of two people in marriage creates a strong spiritual bond. Yet it is as fragile as any other earthly covenant characterized by emotional attachment. The tether is too often frayed by circumstances; once it breaks, the "oneness" is gone. Even the best earthly union is only valid until death.

Our union with Christ is in the deepest sense an unbreakable, lasting covenant. The joy and strength we receive from joining our spirit with the living God lasts through eternity. We become one in the Spirit with our own Creator. He loves us so much that He reaches down in grace to pull us in to Him. We must never lose sight of the glorious truth that allowing people to become one with Him was His choice. He wants us to participate in His reality.

He Is Enough

You are complete in Him, who is the head
of all principality and power.
COLOSSIANS 2:10 NKJV

Our lives are infused, filled, and complete with the Master of order, time, and place. It may seem impossible to fully appreciate our completeness in Christ, but imagine what life would be like if we had no awareness of Jesus' power and desire to provide everything that we need to reflect His glory. His offer of the opportunity to be complete in Him is a genuine demonstration of what He is prepared to share with us—which is everything.

His authority over evil becomes part of our new identity as we discover the freedom we have to access His power. We have been reborn into a privileged state of relationship with God that leaves us wanting for nothing. In our everyday lives, we can tap in to the authority He has given us. We no longer have to settle for less; we have it all—all that Jesus is.

The Gift of Reprieve

There is therefore now no condemnation
to those who are in Christ Jesus.
ROMANS 8:1 NKJV

Every human being who has ever lived should be permanently branded as guilty of a life of sin and disobedience. But because of our relationship with Jesus, God has removed the offending imprint that marked us as sinners. God's plan in all this is weighed heavily in our favor; He has given us much more than He asks us to give in return. By removing the guilty brand from us, He has given us the freedom to walk in the fullness of life here on earth and later in heaven.

The opportunity we have been given to be renewed, transformed, and lifted up is one we don't deserve. But now, because we have chosen Jesus, He showers on us the gifts of pardon and freedom from shame and guilt. We can walk each day in the light of amnesty. We are forgiven!

Dispel the Darkness

"You are the light of the world. A city that is set on a hill cannot be hidden."
MATTHEW 5:14 NKJV

When was the last time you felt as though you were a beacon in the darkness? Most of our lives are spent searching for a light that will show us the way out of our own circumstances. We aren't always aware that people look to us to be the bright spot that will guide them to God. Many of us would much rather hide, thinking we couldn't possibly have any light to offer.

If we have the love of Christ in us, we are light to the world. There is no way to hide an illumination of that magnitude. We may feel ashamed because we think our light is so dim, but remember: It's not our dim light but the brilliant, reflected light of the glory of God that others see.

So go ahead and shine. It's His light anyway.

Always Present

Do you not know that you are the temple of God
and that the Spirit of God dwells in you?
1 CORINTHIANS 3:16 NKJV

God has trusted us to carry His Spirit in the most fragile container—our bodies. It's up to us to determine what kind of container we will be. If His Spirit dwells in us and we maintain our container spiritually, God uses us to spread the good news. But what if we are weak, lifeless, or broken? How effective can we be? If we claim to have the Spirit of God in us, we need to make sure we use our "vessels"—our bodies—in ways that are pleasing to God.

We have been given the ultimate gift of cohabitation with the almighty God. This is a gift to be treasured and revealed to others daily. Our life in the world needs to always be aligned with our life with God.

Beauty of the Heart

"People look at the outward appearance,
but the Lord looks at the heart."
1 Samuel 16:7 niv

As we grow into womanhood, we come up against issues such as insecurity, body image, desire for love, and many other internal struggles. Our standard for measure is usually the world's standards, and we are too easily drawn into measuring ourselves against that false benchmark.

We can free ourselves from the impossible standard the world creates by looking to the truth of God's plan for us. That means accepting ourselves as He made us and stopping our relentless pursuit for peace apart from Him. Our longing for love is satisfied in His perfect design for our individual destiny. Think about that. How can we be concerned about what the world thinks of us when the Creator of the universe thinks the world of us? Jesus is our standard, and in Him we always measure up.

Choose Your Words

The tongue has the power of life and death.

Proverbs 18:21 niv

Our words can bring us down to the depths of despair. Despite what we know to be true about our state of grace, we can destroy our confidence and joy by listening to negative self-talk. It grieves the heart of God to hear His daughters slip under the weight of harmful words. Even those near to us are affected by what we say.

But we have also been shown the power of positive words. Speaking the truth about God's love, forgiveness, favor, and mercy can give new life to our spirit, new inspiration to our soul. When we ask God to guard our tongue, we can be assured that He will give us uplifting words to speak to ourselves and those around us. His life-giving vocabulary has the power to lift us above our circumstances and transform our attitude.

Deeper Union

"In him we live and move and have our being."
Acts 17:28 NIV

Is there a better place to exist than "in Him"—in Christ? In Christ we can survive even the most horrendous circumstances. When we are joined with Him at the very core of our being, His Spirit and ours work together to bring about positive results on earth.

How do we explain this union? Words are seldom sufficient and may not come across as believable to others. We have little choice but to live it out. When we surrender everything to God, we are able to live and move and have our being in Him. Our life with Christ is more than just a casual relationship, and it adds to our lives more than just superficial joys. When we let Christ live through us, others see the results—and suddenly our union with Christ becomes believable.

Power over Fear

God has not given us a spirit of fear, but of power and of love and of a sound mind.

2 TIMOTHY 1:7 NKJV

Nothing will compromise a sound mind faster than fear will. The power that fear has over us is far reaching and fast moving. God has given us specific warnings against letting fear destroy our faith, trust, and passions; He knows how quickly and completely fear can disrupt our thoughts, our plans, and our hopes.

The spirit of fear is especially prevalent when our well-being or our comfortable lives are threatened. Is my husband having an affair? Will my sister survive the operation? What if God calls me to preach in Iran? Our thoughts become clouded and confused, and even ridiculous at times. But God has promised us a sound mind. His powerful hand can crush the spirit of fear and restore the sanity we once had. There is simply no room for fear in a life that is surrendered to God.

You Can Do It

He has made us competent as ministers of a new covenant.
2 CORINTHIANS 3:6 NIV

When God has a job for us to do, He equips us for the task. We don't need to depend on our own strength, pumping up our abilities to meet the task. God has graciously given us all we need to work out His will for our lives. That includes the challenge of spiritual growth; He has provided everything required for us to achieve maturity in our life with Christ.

You may doubt your competence, but God would not have led you to participate in the ministry of His kingdom if He had any doubt that you were able to complete the assignment. In calling you to share in the new covenant, He has shown His confidence and trust in your ability to exercise the gifts He has given you. Consider this question: Who knows more about what you are capable of—you or God?

Heavenly Servants

Angels are only servants—spirits sent to care for people who will inherit salvation.

HEBREWS 1:14 NLT

As if God's Spirit is not enough, as if He hasn't already provided us with all the help and protection we'll ever need, He also sends His angels to care for us. Though we can't see them, they are a constant presence in our lives, sent by the Father to watch over us.

When you feel alone, you can be assured you are not. Not only is God always with you, but also He has surrounded you with a team of angels whose one mission is to serve you. God has instructed that team to do His will concerning you. This is how important you are to Him. How can you not be secure in His love when you know how far His reach extends? Even the angels know how much He loves you, and they are already standing guard over you.

As He Loves

"As I have loved you, so you must love one another."

JOHN 13:34 NIV

Is it possible for humans to love the way God does? His perfect love is unconditional and involves the unthinkable sacrifice of His only Son. But no human being can achieve perfection in any area, let alone in the difficult area of loving others.

But how close can we come to that ideal? If we truly love God, then truly loving others starts with seeing the image of God in them—in the good, the bad, the ugly, everyone who has ever hurt us, and everyone else who has ever lived. It requires embracing everyone and not excluding anyone.

We are in the center of God's will when we serve others in the power of His love. Despite our objection that we can't possibly love this woman or that man, the truth is that we can access the power of God to love everyone, even the unlovable.

A Good Test

You know that when your faith is tested,
your endurance has a chance to grow.
JAMES 1:3 NLT

Good parents turn every test into a lesson to help their child on the path to maturity. Teachers test students to make sure they've learned their lessons well. Medical personnel perform tests to determine what is going on inside the human body. Tests are not necessarily fun and can cause significant anxiety. But tests, no matter how difficult, are an important way to discover problem areas and measure improvement.

Tests of faith can be especially discouraging when we face a challenge without a clear right or wrong answer. Trusting God suddenly becomes critical and imperative; we have nowhere else to turn for guidance that will help us pass the test and advance toward spiritual maturity. God wants us to pass; He wants us to experience a better outcome from our challenges, one that will result in lasting spiritual growth.

Receive His Gifts

Let us come boldly to the throne of our gracious God.
There we will receive his mercy, and we will find
grace to help us when we need it most.
HEBREWS 4:16 NLT

What a gift it is to be invited before the very throne of God! When trials, hardship, emotional pain, or sin threaten to rob us of our peace, we have a standing invitation to enter His presence, where He will shower us with mercy and grace. This offering of hope amid traumatic circumstances and in our chaotic mental state is undeserved, yet God freely extends it to us out of His great love for us.

God's invitation provides much more than a refuge from the world. When we come before His throne in the boldness of a confident child approaching her earthly father, He stretches out His arm of protection and covers us with mercy and grace just when we've reached the end of our own efforts.

He Hears

I cried to my God for help.
From his temple he heard my voice.
Psalm 18:6 NIV

There are days, and sometimes nights, when God seems too far away to hear your cries for help. You feel as if you're hanging on the edge of a cliff with no breath to scream. Small pressures have turned into one big one, and you need to be rescued. You're not alone in that; we all need to be rescued from time to time.

But God does hear. Not only that, He acts on our behalf with regard to anything that causes concern for us in our daily lives. He knows the peril of living in a world of temptation and strife. He takes seriously the cries of His children. He is never far away—and He is always close enough to reach out and touch us in our need.

Even in the Valleys

That is why we never give up. Though our bodies are dying, our spirits are being renewed every day.
2 Corinthians 4:16 NLT

When we stay the course, when we hold tightly to the promises of God, we are rewarded with renewed strength each day. Best of all, we reach the ultimate goal—God gets the praise and glory for our victory. It doesn't matter if our physical bodies are beginning to give out; there are many ways other than the physical to persevere in our walk with God.

In trying times, we have the opportunity to display our dependence on Him. Long after we have seriously considered giving up, He remains with us, holding us up and showing the world the reward for depending on Him. That reward is evidenced every single day, as He renews our spirit and infuses us with the strength to go on.

Grateful for the Light

Your word is a lamp for my feet, a light on my path.

Psalm 119:105 niv

No one likes the feeling of stumbling in the darkness. The absence of light induces fear, insecurity, and sometimes absolute terror. We're afraid to take a step in any direction, and we imagine all kinds of scary things lurking in the shadows, just waiting to trip us up.

Even a tiny flame—the flicker of a candle or the strike of a match—can provide enough light to help us see better. But God doesn't stop there; in our darkness, He offers us a lamp to light our way—His Word. His light shines not just in our room, our private lives, but also on the path we need to follow to accomplish His will in our lives. That light enables us to move forward in the way we should go, perfectly illuminating our walk with Him.

Helper Forever

"I will ask the Father, and he will give you another advocate to help you and be with you forever—the Spirit of truth."
John 14:16–17 NIV

Can you imagine the confusion the disciples experienced when Jesus told them He was going away but that another would come to comfort and help them forever? They had depended on Jesus for their spiritual guidance and had learned about a Father who was just beginning to become real to them. Who would help them now?

No one wants to be alone—even if they say they do. We were not created to be alone. God made us social beings, dependent on one another, dependent on Him. Even after the Holy Spirit revealed Himself to them, it took the disciples awhile to experience the Spirit's comfort. But Jesus sent the Comforter for you, too, and you can experience His comfort, counsel, and guidance immediately—even now. He is closer than you can ever imagine.

Blessed Equation

May our Lord Jesus Christ himself and God our Father, who loved us and by his grace gave us eternal encouragement and good hope.
2 Thessalonians 2:16 niv

Notice the key words in this scripture: love, grace, encouragement, and hope. They cover the pattern of God's working in our lives. Through His love, God gives us the grace we need to overcome our sinful human nature. When God reminds us of that grace, He encourages us in ways the world cannot understand. When we're encouraged, we can see the light at the end of our struggle—the hope we have in Christ.

Hope is the response we express that captures the attention of the world we live in. People are longing for hope, and we are part of the plan God created to reach them with that hope. That plan starts with His love and His character, and ends with hope, His promise that everything will work out for the best—regardless of what happens in the meantime.

He Knows How to Care

"As one whom his mother comforts,
so I will comfort you."
ISAIAH 66:13 NKJV

A caring mother's love, the touch of her hand, and her soothing ways are never forgotten. Long into adulthood we recall our mother's cool caress on our fevered brow or soft kiss on the top of our head. The connection between mother and child can be a strong one, and especially important when a little one needs reassurance and comfort.

God knows how to envelop us in an even greater kind of comfort than that of a loving parent. He sees deep into our need and knows just how to minister healing and love. We can come to Him when we are weary, afraid, or hurt, and He will soothe our troubled hearts with kindness and compassion. He is always there for His children, making everything right again.

Catch Me!

When I said, "My foot is slipping,"
your unfailing love, LORD, supported me.
PSALM 94:18 NIV

As your guide, the Father watches each step you take. He sees the path ahead and points the way to the best foothold, the one that will keep you from falling. In the heat of the climb to spiritual maturity, you may panic, fearing you will fall and hit the bottom of a great crevasse. But even as your foot falters and the rocks crumble beneath you, God reaches you just in time to secure your step.

A sure footing is wonderfully comforting. Knowing that God watches each move we make in our climb is even more reassuring. His love and support keep us moving upward, reaching higher than we first dreamed possible. He knows how quickly we can tire, and He is always there to keep us steady as we reach for that higher calling, our role in bringing about the kingdom of God on earth.

Permanent Adoption

"No, I will not abandon you
as orphans—I will come to you."
John 14:18 NLT

Even if our earthly father has died or has abandoned us, none of us will ever be fatherless. Our heavenly Father, by His very nature, cannot and will not leave us to wander the earth alone. We may take on the attitude of an orphan, rejecting His adoption, but He is always watching us, waiting for us to recognize His presence. He patiently woos us into His forever family.

This is the secure relationship that exists only between God and His children. All other relationships end when one party dies. But we need never fear that He will disappear from our lives. He can't, because He is and was and forever will be. We can rejoice in the solid family tie that is ours in Christ Jesus!

Speak God's Words

We urge you, brothers and sisters, warn those who are idle and disruptive, encourage the disheartened, help the weak, be patient with everyone.

1 THESSALONIANS 5:14 NIV

What image comes to mind when you think of the idle, the disheartened, and the weak as a group? Very likely, the image is that of the homeless, many of whom suffer from mental illness to varying degrees. As women, we may feel compassion for them, but fear often keeps us from speaking God's healing truth into their lives.

But discernment and wisdom from the Holy Spirit can overcome our fear. When we obey the genuine urging of the Holy Spirit to reach out in love to those who need help, we not only minister to them; we too are uplifted and encouraged. Speaking the words out loud to another person, we hear them for ourselves. When they are God's words, they have power to heal and make all things new, for both the one who hears and the one who speaks.

Choose Gladness

When anxiety was great within me,
your consolation brought me joy.
Psalm 94:19 NIV

Have you ever felt your mood change suddenly? Your day is going badly, and you've settled into the dumps. Then your child says something funny or you get good news. Now you feel better—you can laugh and feel the joy of a burden lifted. By the end of the day you're able to be thankful for the blessings that have come your way.

The comfort Jesus brings to your circumstances will lift you higher than you're able to climb on your own. He senses your negative emotions and wants to bring a lightness to your heart that will overcome the depression caused by your worry and doubt; He sees the anxiety etched on your face and wants to free you from your cares. Turn to Jesus and allow Him to change your mood so suddenly that it will bring joy to your soul.

A Helping Hand

Worry weighs a person down;
an encouraging word cheers a person up.
Proverbs 12:25 NLT

Once we have experienced depression to any degree, we realize how wonderful it is to be free of it. Someone comes along with a word of hope, and we can see the light of Jesus in the distance, pulling us along, back to a right mindset. Sometimes just a smile or hug is enough to reflect the love of Jesus we desperately need.

Then it's our turn to reach out to someone else. By sharing a kind and encouraging word, our own healing can be accomplished. Helping someone out by sharing our personal experiences—with depression, for instance—can change our own attitude. When we ease the anxiety of someone else, we go a long way toward easing our own anxiety. In fact, caring for others may be the best method of self-care that we will ever know.

Imagine the Joy

Some men brought to him a paralyzed man,
lying on a mat. When Jesus saw their faith, he said
to the man, "Take heart, son; your sins are forgiven."
MATTHEW 9:2 NIV

The paralyzed man was blessed to have such devoted friends to carry him into the presence of Jesus. By the mercy of God, he was forgiven on the spot. Perhaps he might have been satisfied with that, but then Jesus healed him. Forgiveness and healing were new experiences for this man.

As Christians we know the price that was paid for us to be forgiven of our sins. How can we not be encouraged? We should be continually thankful for our salvation—so much so that we can rejoice even when we aren't healed. We can be comforted in knowing God has come into our lives and changed us. That's enough blessing to last for eternity.

Be Free

He has sent me to comfort the brokenhearted
and to proclaim that captives will be released
and prisoners will be freed.
Isaiah 61:1 NLT

Imagine a prisoner sitting in a foreign jail waiting to be freed but fearful he could spend the rest of his life paying for his mistake—or possibly paying for something he never even did. He hears good news from home saying he has an advocate working on his behalf to free him. He looks around his cell, and the thought of his release fills him with hope and gratitude for his rescuer.

Jesus is such an advocate for us, and He never fails to free us from the prison our sin has made for us. He holds the keys to the prison cell, and He offers us a chance to start over. This is our good news from home! This is cause for celebration—and for encouragement to our tired bodies, aching hearts, and empty souls.

Freely Receive, Freely Give

"Blessed are the merciful,
for they shall obtain mercy."
MATTHEW 5:7 NKJV

How soon we forget the magnitude of God's mercy in our lives! We, the undeserving, have been on the receiving end of God's favor after we've botched things up, but what do we do when others mess up and need our understanding, our grace, our mercy? Do we withhold what they need? Do we judge or condemn them? Or do we become the love of Christ in their lives? When we deny others the mercy we have graciously been given, we miss the opportunity to become like Christ—and more importantly, like Christ to those who need Him most.

God offers us a second chance if only we will extend the same undeserved favor God has shown us. As we participate in this cycle of grace, we are a part of a wonderful exchange. Someone is waiting to give you mercy today—receive it, and then give it away.

Refreshing Love

Your love has given me great joy and encouragement,
because you, brother, have refreshed the
hearts of the Lord's people.
PHILEMON 1:7 NIV

We belong to the family of God and are called according to His purpose. Our interaction in this family and beyond is not only essential to our personal growth, it also spills over into the lives of others as we show them the love of God. Answering this call brings harmony and unity to the Body of Christ. Those who receive our acts of kindness are partners in our blessings—and our obedience ends up encouraging us as well.

The chain of encouragement is life giving and life altering. It pleases the Lord to see we are about His business, and our spirit in turn is strengthened by knowing we are in the center of His will. As we seek to bring refreshment to others, our own heart is refreshed.

He's Here

Immediately he spoke to them and said,
"Take courage! It is I. Don't be afraid."
MARK 6:50 NIV

Learning to recognize God's presence helps us trust Him and have the assurance that we can accomplish what He asks. We come to know His ways and sense His guidance as we spend more time with Him. When we welcome Him into our lives, we discover that He wants to walk beside us every day.

When we open our spiritual eyes to see Jesus working in us, we find the courage, confidence, and motivation we thought we lacked. We don't have to be afraid of our weaknesses. We can move forward in any battle with Him beside us; Jesus dispels the darkness and lights our path so we won't give in to fear or lies. We don't have to worry about our deficiencies, because we are depending on Him. We have His courage inside us!

Lift Up Another

If your gift is to encourage others, be encouraging.

ROMANS 12:8 NLT

All who are part of the Body of Christ have been given a gift. Some are teachers, some prophets—and some are encouragers. Where would the Body of Christ, or the world, be without encouragers? We can't have too many! We need extra comfort and new perspectives amid the harsh realities of today's world. Encouragement helps ease the pain and suffering that all too many people are living with.

We are called to be encouragers even if encouragement is not our special gift. It should automatically flow from the love of Christ living in us, giving us the power to strengthen God's people. It doesn't take much; a smile, a few encouraging words, or simply our presence in a time of need can be enough to help someone climb out of a pit of discouragement. Being an encouragement is a simple way to change our world for the better.

As Unto Him

Serve wholeheartedly, as if you were serving the Lord, not people.
Ephesians 6:7 niv

Women have a special aptitude for serving. We love to see the smiles on the faces of those to whom we show hospitality. But some people never show their appreciation—or worse, they complain about the things we have done to please them. In the presence of those who are hostile or indifferent despite our efforts at serving them, it's important to remember that we are to treat them as if they are Christ Himself. This changes the game considerably. We have to adopt a new attitude, one that is designed to show people who Jesus really is.

We have a divine connection with the Lord when we embrace servanthood. He was the greatest servant of all, and His example in sacrifice and service set the tone for His entire ministry on earth. This is the ministry we are called to. We serve as if we are serving Him, which is a remarkable way to live and one that mirrors the heart of God. We were made for this!

Care More

Is anyone among you in trouble? Let them pray.
Is anyone happy? Let them sing songs of praise.
James 5:13 NIV

The understanding of what we want and the realities of what we get are hard to bridge. Most of us experience disappointment and unhappiness when our desires aren't fulfilled. But when things go our way, we feel like singing. How do we make sure we never experience disappointment? Is it possible to be happy in all circumstances?

Yes, it is—when we focus our attention on Jesus and not on our desires. We may occasionally fall back into the old habit of always wanting things to go our way, but Jesus wants us to deepen our desire for Him. This is how we avoid disappointment—by caring so much about Jesus and His plan for us that we are able to ignore our wish lists. Living this way frees us from the bondage of desire—and finds us singing joyful songs of praise.

Dry Your Eyes

"Blessed are those who mourn,
for they shall be comforted."
MATTHEW 5:4 NKJV

By God's design, we are emotional creatures. We show respect for our deceased loved ones and express our pain when we mourn for them. Because every relationship is unique and every individual experiences grief in a unique way, some people mourn for a longer time than others do. But there comes a time when mourning must end if we are to experience emotional wholeness.

Jesus promised that we would be comforted during our time of mourning. We can choose not to accept that comfort, of course; no one will try to force us to accept it. But relief from our sorrow will come sooner if we allow God—and other people—to be a comfort to us. Unending grief paralyzes us, because our constant focus on ourselves and the sorrow we feel keeps us from moving on with our lives. Let Jesus soothe your pain—and experience the joy of serving God and others once again.

Friends of Jesus

"Now you are my friends, since I have told you everything the Father told me."
JOHN 15:15 NLT

The pain of a friend's rebuke slices deep into our hearts. A betrayal can become an insurmountable pile of resentment that ends a relationship. Indifference may be the only response you receive from someone you thought cared about you. These are among the pitfalls and risks of giving your heart to a friend.

Our friendship with Jesus is made of stronger stuff. His commitment is never compromised, and His attributes of loyalty, steadfastness, and extravagant love never leave us wanting or disappointed. He chooses us, and we can find joy in knowing He will never betray us, ignore us, or cause us pain in any way at all. We can rest in the knowledge that if all our earthly friends abandoned us, we will never be friendless. We will always have Jesus.

Big Dreams

Sarah laughed to herself as she thought, "After I am worn out and my lord is old, will I now have this pleasure?"

GENESIS 18:12 NIV

We all know some dreams come true—but this one? Nonsense. To Sarah, this promise seemed impossible, more difficult to fulfill than the parting of the Red Sea. Even though she had made it clear to God that her heart's desire was for a child, and even though Abraham had been promised the blessing of descendants who would populate the earth, neither Sarah nor Abraham believed the prophecy that she would bear a child in her old age.

But Sarah did conceive, and she bore the son she was promised. God is in the business of delivering on His pledges. We may not know when or where they'll come to pass, but we can take courage in knowing they will. We may laugh as Sarah did, but not even our scoffing can thwart God's purposes. If He wants a thing to happen, you can be certain it will.

His Strength in Me

I will boast all the more gladly about my weaknesses,
so that Christ's power may rest on me.
2 CORINTHIANS 12:9 NIV

We've heard this verse preached many times, and the message is clear: Christ is strong in our weakness. But is this something we should brag about? Yes, it is. Anything that proves the presence and power of God living in us is well worth boasting about. This is not so much about humility, although that's part of the process, but it is more about the joy of seeing Christ working through us.

We are chosen to be His temple. But in our frailty and flaws, we would be worthless without His power. He restores us and patches up all the cracks in our form, making us the perfect receptacle. We need to give Him the glory for mending us and making us whole—especially when others see the end result and are drawn to His power.

The Real You

You created my inmost being; you knit me together in my mother's womb.

Psalm 139:13 NIV

No one knows you the way the Father does. He created you to be who you are; He watched over you and guarded your life even before you were born. He welcomed you into His family, and He will love you throughout eternity.

It simply does not matter what others say about you, whether it's based on the truth—maybe you did do some of the things they said!—or it's nothing more than an unfounded rumor. Nothing can ever change the fact that you are who your Creator says you are. Since coming to Him, you have become a whole new person. He is on your side and always will be. He knows everything there is to know about you, and He has deemed you worthy of His love. Rejoice in the truth about who you are in Christ. Embrace the way He made you. He knew what He was doing.

Share His Glory

This is the secret: Christ lives in you.
This gives you assurance of sharing his glory.
COLOSSIANS 1:27 NLT

Our heart is the home of the Son of God. He takes up residence in us, offering to share the riches of heaven with us. Why is this a secret? Maybe it's because we don't quite understand the significance of Christ's life in us; we're afraid that it's too good to be true.

Most of us have no problem sharing this secret with those we minister to. But cementing it in our own hearts is often a more difficult task. Saying the words isn't enough; we must learn to absorb the wonderful gifts and blessings that come from God's outpouring of grace. But who are we that the Son of God would choose us? All that matters is that He did choose us, and we can rejoice that He made that choice.

Solid Ground

He will be the sure foundation for your times,
a rich store of salvation and wisdom and knowledge.
Isaiah 33:6 niv

Could you use a bit more stability in your life? Or a sure foundation? How about some wisdom and knowledge? In times of trouble, we cry out for just those things, but what do we do in times of abundance or peace? When things are going our way, we take our storehouse for granted. Our foundation in Christ—and the rich store of salvation, wisdom, and knowledge—is there all the time, and yet we panic when things don't go our way.

When we lack the wisdom we need for tough situations, God is ready to get us up to speed by giving us access to all that He is. And that, of course, is all we need.

He Will Not Be Moved

The Lord's plans stand firm forever;
his intentions can never be shaken.
Psalm 33:11 NLT

God's kingdom, down to the smallest detail, cannot collapse. When it seems as if life is crumbling all around us, we know that nothing can be moved from His plan. He knows what we need and how to fix our brokenness, because His intentions toward us were formed before we were born. His plan is a better design than we could possibly invent for ourselves.

His plan for us isn't affected by our indecisiveness or reluctance to obey, nor is the way He deals with us when we refuse to listen. His patience outlasts our disobedience, because His plan for us is solid. His intentional love and grace stand forever. When you feel shaken, lean on His arm and let Him take you to a safe place.

Think Eternally

Command those who are rich in this present world
not to be arrogant nor to put their hope in wealth,
which is so uncertain, but to put their hope in God.
1 Timothy 6:17 niv

On what do you fix your hope? Do you mistakenly trust in the things in your world? All of that will perish someday—and then what will become of your security?

We have forgotten that mere things represent much less than God wants for us. We give them too much credit for making us happy. Things don't have the power to change us. They only keep us tied to the physical world. The spiritual activity in our lives is what brings abundance, security, and permanence.

Reaching for the intangibles like holiness, charity, and wisdom takes us to a deeper level of existence—and that's something God wants us to experience.

Find the Hills

After sending them home, he went up
into the hills by himself to pray.
MATTHEW 14:23 NLT

We often hear young mothers telling tales of endless days with no time for themselves. Many of us lived those days, days when we longed for one whole minute of silent contemplation. Busy households are often run by women who can't seem to find time to find time!

Jesus had a similar problem. Everywhere He went there were crowds of people wanting something from Him. He tried to find solitude, but most of the time it eluded Him. Even the King of the universe struggled to have time to Himself.

When we take advantage of the very things that will keep us going in busy times, we function better because our spirit is filled. We need to give ourselves permission to take a break and hear from God. We need time to simply be still.

He Is for You

You hem me in behind and before,
and you lay your hand upon me.
PSALM 139:5 NIV

It's comforting when a friend or loved one tries to protect you, whether it's from the unkindness of another or a very real danger. But no matter how hard they try, they can't protect you the way God can. When He lays His hand of protection on you, there is nothing that can break through it. The fortress of His love surrounds you completely, leaving no cracks for the arrows of evil to get through. We may not be able to see the spiritual armor we're wearing, but we know it's there because God is the one who placed it on us to begin with.

In times of trouble and panic, close your eyes and visualize His protection. You can lean on His promise to stand with you in the many battles of life. He covers you on every side and leads you safely through every hostile situation.

A New Perception

I pray that the eyes of your heart may be enlightened in order that you may know the hope to which he has called you.

Ephesians 1:18 niv

The greatest kind of imagination is that which is poured straight into our minds by God. It enables us to connect with His creativity and enjoy a new perspective on whatever we experience. This kind of "seeing" is part of going deeper with God, seeing through His eyes, soaking in the hope of what's to come.

God has called us to understand and implement the kind of expectancy that bears fruit in our lives. This is a high calling and one that is not hidden, as we may have thought. He awakens us to all the possibilities we have dared not consider. As our minds are filled with His light and understanding, we experience all that He has promised us.

Shout It Out

It is good to proclaim your unfailing love in
the morning, your faithfulness in the evening.
PSALM 92:2 NLT

Studies have shown that the more frequently we say something out loud, the more we tend to believe it. But as Christians, we didn't need a study to confirm that; we know that proclaiming the love of God right out loud strengthens our faith. God proves His faithfulness throughout our day, and one of the best ways we can show our gratitude for that is by praising Him. Something special happens when we give God credit and honor for His goodness and mercy.

Our gratitude overflows from our heart then spreads to the hearing ears of those who need hope. Our declaration of His loving-kindness is a testament of His working in our lives. And the benefits of praising Him come right back to us; we reap the joy that comes from giving Him glory.

By His Hand

No weapon forged against you will prevail,
and you will refute every tongue that accuses you.
Isaiah 54:17 NIV

Words of accusation can cut deep into our hearts, especially when we have worked hard on a relationship that has suddenly fallen apart and the other person has turned against us without provocation. It seems so unfair that while we are doing our best to accomplish the Lord's will in our lives, we are falsely accused. It's a heartbreak that most of us have had to endure, sometimes alone.

The promises of God are our shield in all circumstances. Our comfort in times of emotional pain is in knowing He has been with us in the hardest of times, defending our honor and sustaining our dignity. And even though victory may sometimes be hard to see, we have God's assurance that the victory is indeed ours.

Resist the Charge

"The battle is not yours, but God's."
2 Chronicles 20:15 niv

You can see it coming—another battle on the horizon. It's headed straight for you, and you wonder how you will ever be able to fight this one. You're tired and confused, unable to formulate a plan of action. Fear cuts like a knife through your heart, and it seems that winning this one will be impossible.

Still, we quickly take up our sword and start swinging. We volunteer for an army we weren't meant to join, a battle we weren't meant to fight. God is our commanding officer in every battle, and that means we can lay down our weapons because we know that He will always be victorious over our enemies.

We can rest in the knowledge that He will finish the fight with His mighty power. God is in charge; wait for your orders before you take up the sword.

Time Away

He lets me rest in green meadows;
he leads me beside peaceful streams.
PSALM 23:2 NLT

Would you like to take a walk with the Lord and meander through a meadow to a cool stream? You could talk with Him, telling Him all your troubles and listening to His words of wisdom and comfort. He would encourage you in your struggles and nourish your soul. This is the escape you dream of on long, trying days.

Jesus is waiting to go with you on this relaxing retreat from the world. You only need to find a quiet place and invite Him to join you for this time of spiritual refreshment. As you make time to spend with Him, He will lead you to that peaceful state of mind that dispels all chaos. It's like a little vacation from the stress of your life—and you return with renewed energy and a sense of deep restoration.

He Never Quits Giving

Out of his fullness we have all received
grace in place of grace already given.
JOHN 1:16 NIV

Where can we go to find an endless supply of all that we need? It's a waste of time to dream of such a resource, because that endless supply is already ours. It's right here, right now, but we foolishly look elsewhere for our needs to be filled. We know that God alone is our resource, for both the necessities of life and those bonus blessings that surprise us when we least expect something good to come our way.

We can lay aside our useless expectations of help from others and put our hope in the one who never fails. We have only tapped the surface of the fullness of His grace. There is so much more for us to experience, so much more He wants to give us.

A Father's Gift

You are no longer a slave, but God's child; and since you are his child, God has made you also an heir.
GALATIANS 4:7 NIV

When you were a child, did your parents give you an allowance? If they did, it was probably based on whether or not you did your chores. You had to earn it. Sometimes you may have felt as though you were a slave to your chores. But oh, how sweet it was to hold that money in your hand! Your parents rewarded you for your obedience.

God has rewarded us too, but with riches beyond our dreams. He has offered to us the gift of His inheritance—as if being called His child wasn't enough! We need never feel as if we are enslaved; He lavishes His blessings on us with no thought to what we must give in return—because without His blessings, we have nothing anyway.

The Best Law

Through Christ Jesus the law of the Spirit who gives life has set you free from the law of sin and death.

ROMANS 8:2 NIV

We all like laws when they apply to someone else. When our freedom to do what we want is restricted by rules and regulations, we complain that we don't deserve that kind of treatment. But the guy down the street? Well, that's another matter entirely. He needs those restrictions. We obviously don't.

The world says it's okay to ignore the boundaries of a conventional God and find freedom in what feels good. But we have been freed from the invisible chains of worldly permissiveness, the real chains that bind us; what the world calls freedom, we recognize as bondage to sin. The law of the Spirit is the only law that truly offers freedom. It's the one law that releases us from prison rather than locks us up in it.

The Great Exchange

"Blessed are those who trust in the Lord and have made the Lord their hope and confidence. They are like trees planted along a riverbank, with roots that reach deep into the water."

Jeremiah 17:7–8 NLT

Where else will you find the great exchange of blessing for trust in a relationship? Our trust in God is a sign to Him that we are in agreement with His plan for us. Our gain is the blessings that come from surrendering to His will. Blessings such as peace, joy, wisdom, vision, favor, and spiritual health are the ingredients that create the encouragement we need to succeed in our Christian walk.

Trusting God and becoming grounded in Him provides the nourishment we need to grow spiritually. Once we have placed our hope and confidence in God, we can begin to draw from the deep wells of His wisdom—and then we are well on our way toward spiritual maturity.

A New Way to Focus

You will keep in perfect peace all who trust in you,
all whose thoughts are fixed on you!
ISAIAH 26:3 NLT

All the distractions of your busy life keep your mind buzzing with responsibilities, duties, chore lists, and upsetting conversations. It's difficult to sort through the negative and find the positive energy you need to function. Peace is somewhere out there on the periphery, but it remains just beyond your reach. Your concentration comes and goes, and so does your hope. And finally, one day you realize your problem: You have put your faith in things that are temporal and unreliable.

Perfect peace is waiting for you. Keep your mind on the scriptures that encourage you, and seek a new biblical focus for each day. As you see your newfound focus work on your behalf, trusting God with all the details of your life may very well become routine—and a pleasant routine at that.

Exchanged Life

I have been crucified with Christ and I
no longer live, but Christ lives in me.
GALATIANS 2:20 NIV

All the knowledge and practical experience we accumulate in a lifetime will not profit us eternally. Neither will our physical accomplishments or advanced mental abilities help create the kingdom of God on their own. It's going to take something more—or something less. It's going to take death to self.

Does dying to self sound like anything but loss? The world sees it as loss. But when we die to self, letting Christ rule our hearts and minds, we have lost nothing but gained everything.

Christ's sacrifice was an example to us of how the apparent worst loss ever—the death of Jesus—became the greatest gain we could ever imagine. We can now live a new life of union with Christ. His life in us is pure, holy, and productive, offering us a sense of freedom and fulfillment that we can't experience any other way.

Change Your Mind

Fix your thoughts on what is true, and honorable, and right, and pure, and lovely, and admirable. Think about things that are excellent and worthy of praise.

PHILIPPIANS 4:8 NLT

When your mind is filled with negativity and dark thoughts, there is no room for light and joy. The medical profession has told us for years about the influence of our minds on our physical health. Our energy levels are lower, and our ability to fight off invasive infections drops off. It's more healthy mentally and physically to keep our thoughts and attitudes positive.

There is so much about God and His blessings to focus on that there's just no need for us to ever dwell on things that bring us down. But sometimes, for any number of reasons, we choose to entertain negative thoughts. We need to remember that encouragement is always available, and we can choose to listen to encouraging words and think positive thoughts—regardless of our circumstances.

He Planned It

We are God's handiwork, created in Christ Jesus to do good works, which God prepared in advance for us to do.

Ephesians 2:10 niv

Doing good isn't just the right thing to do—it's our destiny, our purpose. What better satisfaction can there be than knowing we are living the life we were created to live? Good works are a reflection of God's character in us. When we are filled with Him, we can't help but share it. While we bless another, we are blessed. When we encourage another, we are encouraged.

It was God's design that we extend His provision to a world in need. We are His hand extended, and when we are part of His plan, we have the added benefit of being able to see how graciously He works. There is no lack of opportunity to do good in the name of Jesus—and doing good is what we were created to do in the first place.

Welcome His Covering

He remembered us in our weakness.
His faithful love endures forever.
Psalm 136:23 NLT

Times of weakness make us want to hide and pretend nothing is wrong. We don't want anyone, especially God, to see how vulnerable we are or how weak we have been. The very thing we need is what we shun—love and acceptance. If we let others in and allow them to get close to us, they may find out who we are inside and discover our weaknesses. We're afraid they won't love us anymore.

The beauty of God is that He loves us despite our weaknesses and mistakes—and He knows more about them than we do! We never have to be afraid that He won't love us anymore. We don't need to hide from Him or pretend to be someone we are not. He loves us with His forever love.

He Forgives and Forgets

"I—yes, I alone—will blot out your sins for my own sake and will never think of them again."
ISAIAH 43:25 NLT

Has your reputation or credibility been tarnished by someone who repeatedly brings up your past? You feel as though some things you've done or said will follow you the rest of your life, ruining relationships and leaving you feeling defeated. Maybe you committed a somewhat minor offense against a friend—or maybe you messed up your life and just about everybody else's in a major way. It doesn't matter either way; you just wish everyone could forget who you used to be.

Unlike people, God is able and willing to forgive and forget. He will never throw your past in your face or hold you back from moving forward in your new life. He offers you freedom from the old chains. He sees only your present and your future. You are who He says you are!

It's There for You

I can do all this through him who gives me strength.

PHILIPPIANS 4:13 NIV

Situations don't have to be negative to be difficult. Even in the best of times we need God's help to stay on track. Our bodies fail, and our foggy minds occasionally need a boost of clarity and vitality, but we have at our disposal everything we need to persevere through whatever life throws at us.

When Christ comes to dwell in us, He brings all that He is to our union. When we require wisdom, it's there for the asking. When we need discernment, He lets us see through His eyes. As we struggle to finish the race, His Word provides encouragement. We find new fortitude in knowing He is ready to not only stand beside us but also propel us forward. We may not be able to do it all as the world defines it, but we can do everything that God calls us to do.

Mark of Approval

"Give your servant success today by granting him favor in the presence of this man."
NEHEMIAH 1:11 NIV

We've all heard the expression, "It's not what you know but who you know that counts." The saying suggests how important it is to have a reference, a recommendation, or a word of praise from an influential person—someone who wants us to do well and is willing to help.

In spiritual matters that's especially true. Having God on our side provides the best reference and the best approval we can possibly get. He is able to grant us favor and direct us to the people we need to see and the places where we need to go. God opens all the right doors for us. And He does so for one reason—His overwhelming love for us, a love that wants only the best for us.

Hear Him Call

"My sheep listen to my voice; I know them, and they follow me. I give them eternal life, and they shall never perish; no one will snatch them out of my hand."

John 10:27–28 NIV

If you became separated from your guide during a snowy mountain climbing expedition, you could find yourself in a life-threatening situation. You've been depending on him all along to steer you away from the dangerous crevasses. Fear grips your heart as you realize that you could be left in the freezing cold to die. If only you could hear your guide calling your name, you could follow his voice to where he is.

God is our eternal guide. He calls to us when we've lost our way, and if we recognize His voice, we can follow the sound until we are in the safety of His arms. Once we are there, we have all the shelter we need. Nothing can harm us or wrench us from His loving embrace.

Take Refuge

He shall cover you with His feathers,
and under His wings you shall take refuge;
His truth shall be your shield and buckler.
Psalm 91:4 NKJV

When we need covering and a safe place to flee, God's protective arm envelops us under His comforting wings. Like a baby chick, we will venture out again and get into trouble, because we must learn our way in the world. God knows we need sanctuary, and when it's scary and we feel panicky, we always have His hiding place to run to.

There He will share truths from His Word to take with us when we venture out yet again. We pull them out to shield us and hold us steadfast in all our battles. When we return to Him, He soothes our wounds and teaches us how to do better next time. His arms are always ready to receive us—and we always have a safe and secure refuge in His presence.

He Has Overcome

You are of God, little children, and have overcome them, because He who is in you is greater than he who is in the world.
1 JOHN 4:4 NKJV

Sometimes it seems as if the world we live in is conspiring to destroy us. Every time we turn around a new disaster looms on the horizon. And it's not just the distant troubles that concern us—the wars, the famines, the natural disasters. We also face trauma in our personal lives, and we feel as if the difficulties at home will be our undoing.

But according to the Word of God, we are overcomers. We are God's offspring, and we have inherited the weapons—our God-given strength in the Holy Spirit—to take on anything that would rob us of our joy. We need to remind ourselves daily that God is greater than anything that could be thrown at us—and that alone can give us the breathing space we need to endure any situation.

His Eye on You

He will not let your foot slip—he who watches over you will not slumber.
Psalm 121:3 NIV

Ever take your eyes off your toddler for a minute only to turn around and find him about to step off the curb and into the street? You get that sinking feeling when you think about what could have happened if you hadn't caught him in time. It's hard to keep children under our watchful eye every second. After all, we are only human.

Even adults are sometimes like that child, wanting to explore the world but headed for danger. Our heavenly Father never takes His eyes off us. He has us always in His sight. His hand reaches out to protect us even when we aren't paying attention. And unlike humans, He never gets distracted.

Better Than Man's Praise

Charm is deceptive, and beauty is fleeting.
PROVERBS 31:30 NIV

Most people love to have the approval of others, and for young girls that often means the approval of their fathers. It doesn't seem to matter whether the fathers are good or bad at parenting; little girls seem to want to know that they have pleased the first man in their lives. Unfortunately, the standard that is used today to offer approval is too frequently based on appearance and performance. Even good fathers fail to realize how often they praise their daughters for how they look rather than for who they are.

Praise from the world offers temporary satisfaction. We don't need that kind of approval; the only approval we should care about is the approval of our heavenly Father. What could possibly compare with the praise of our Creator? His is the praise that is to be the most prized and treasured.

It's Not Too Much for Him

Jesus looked at them intently and said,
"Humanly speaking, it is impossible.
But with God everything is possible."
MATTHEW 19:26 NLT

Too often, we are crushed under the weight of discouraging impossibilities. Everywhere we look we see difficult situations, broken relationships, or financial burdens that seem to have no solution. Looking through the lens of our human limitations, our hope slips away, and doubt takes its place. The mountain is too big to move.

Jesus recognizes our wavering faith as we look at those mountains. He patiently reminds us that God is the God of possibilities. He created everything and has power over everything that is seen and unseen. As we reinforce this truth in our minds, our faith grows—and we begin to realize how often God makes a "yes" out of our "no." He opens new doors for us every day. We just need to walk through them.

Praise Him

I will extol the Lord with all my heart.

Psalm 111:1 niv

Almighty God created us for His pleasure and offers us fellowship with Him. Out of His great love for us, He adopted us, saved us, and pours out His blessings on us. He shelters us, guides us, and never gives up on us, even when we are at our worst.

How can we possibly return the faith He has in us? He is worthy of our praise and gratitude. We need to set aside our discomfort and pride to declare His loving-kindness and share the good news of His love to all the world. There's no way to repay what He has done for us, but we can bless His name in the presence of others—offering up our thanks to Him and giving Him credit for all that is good in our lives.

Share the Plan

He has enabled us to be ministers of his new covenant.
This is a covenant not of written laws, but of the Spirit.
2 Corinthians 3:6 NLT

When you are feeling down about yourself, one of the best things you can do is listen to the Spirit reminding you of the agreement you have entered into with Christ. He has promoted you to the high position of minister in His plan to save humankind. You are His ambassador, with a calling to declare your faith and His glory.

We are not bound by law to this agreement, but better yet, we are joined in unity with the Holy Spirit who communicates the heart of the Father through us. We are chosen to be part of a bigger plan and can take joy in knowing He trusts us with our special position—in partnership with the living God!

He Takes Your Burdens

Cast all your anxiety on him because he cares for you.
1 Peter 5:7 niv

Climbing a mountain is slow going when you have to pack a load on your back. Each step is labored, and it's hard to enjoy yourself when you feel burdened down with all that weight. You dare not stop to admire the view; you may not want to get going again! There are times when you think you won't make it to the top.

Our worries are useless weight. Yet we pack them up as if we must carry them wherever we go. They ruin our mood, slow us down, and keep our eyes off the one who has offered to carry them for us. God will gladly remove our burdens—perhaps not the circumstances, but the pain they cause—if only we would let Him.

Remember and Sing

Sing, O heavens! Be joyful, O earth! And break out in singing, O mountains! For the Lord has comforted His people, and will have mercy on His afflicted.

Isaiah 49:13 NKJV

Drowning in our misery is the fast track to more misery. Even when things look bleak and hopeless, we have reason to be joyful. God has shown mercy in all our failures. He has lifted us out of past afflictions. Our condition would be unimaginable without His comfort and intervention. If He never did another thing for us, we would still have reason to sing His praise.

When you need encouragement, return to your memories of those times when His gracious hand was resting on you. Think of where you would be without Him. He created beauty from ashes for your good. Praising God—in the bad times as well as the good—is the most positive experience you can have.

Never-Ending Love

"Though the mountains be shaken and the hills be removed, yet my unfailing love for you will not be shaken nor my covenant of peace be removed," says the LORD, who has compassion on you.

ISAIAH 54:10 NIV

Forever is a difficult concept to grasp. We're accustomed to living moment by moment, not thinking too far into the future. How then can we understand how love can last forever? To our finite minds, love is fleeting and changeable. Not so with Almighty God. His love is not temporal; neither does it change with circumstance or failings. We are locked into this love relationship even beyond our time on earth.

Everything else around us may fall apart—our relationships, our careers, our health. But nothing can stop God's love. We can have peace and absolute assurance about that. Even if we can't grasp it, we can rejoice because of it.

His Plan Is Better

Commit to the Lord whatever you do,
and he will establish your plans.
Proverbs 16:3 NIV

God is the great architect of our lives. He knows how our future should be built. Just as we would hand over to a designer the responsibility of drawing up plans for our house, we need to relinquish our plans for the future to God. He customizes them just for us, solidifying our destiny. Giving our plans to God is never a risk, because He already knows the timeline of our lives. That was established even before we were born. He longs to perfect it for you.

When we surrender control of our lives to God, He takes even the minor details and molds them into a complete picture of what our lives were meant to be. Together, we create the wonder of a well-designed life in God. With God in control, guiding our steps, we must never consider the events in our lives to be mere accidents. Each one has a purpose designed specifically for us.

High Above

Those who trust in the LORD will find new strength. They will soar high on wings like eagles. They will run and not grow weary. They will walk and not faint.

ISAIAH 40:31 NLT

The flight of an eagle is a beautiful thing to see. The ease with which eagles ride the wind currents seems effortless and looks exhilarating. Flying high above the troubles of earth, their bird's-eye view of dangers below gives them an advantage over the creatures below. Eagles' wings are designed to withstand the wind that blows against them, and they use that to their advantage.

God offers you this exciting state of soaring bliss. Trusting Him is your ticket to fly high above your present danger. The more you trust, the more successful you'll be at using the currents of life to your advantage. No more fainting! You'll gain strength from soaring.

Choose Courage

"Be strong and courageous. Do not be afraid; do not be discouraged, for the LORD your God will be with you wherever you go."

JOSHUA 1:9 NIV

Fear and discouragement go hand in hand to pull us away from victory. They are powerful forces that affect our daily living. Strength and courage are our defense against such negative elements. We have both at our disposal at all times, because God is with us wherever we are. He brings along all the strength and fortitude we need to defeat negative feelings of fear and doubt.

We don't have to choose fear anymore. We can use the courage God gives us to place ourselves above the thoughts and beliefs that hinder us. Don't just trust the facts of your situation—believe the truth of God's Word for it. At all times and in every situation, you have an advocate in God.

It's Better to Suffer?

It is good for me that I have been afflicted,
that I may learn Your statutes.
Psalm 119:71 NKJV

Life is good. Everything has gone according to your plans, and you are facing no resistance to what you want for your future. How can that be? Well, you've played it safe and taken no risks, eliminating any possibility of discomfort. Things seem to be working well. But when you stack your spiritual depth against that of someone who has been through trials and devastation, you may find you are lacking in maturity.

We grow when we experience affliction. God uses it to deepen our faith, sharpen our dependence on Him, and prove His faithfulness. When we shield ourselves so heavily from hard times, we end up with a shallow faith. We are better off for having risked our peaceful safety in exchange for a depth of maturity that comes from experiencing personal pain.

Stay Connected

"Remain in me, as I also remain in you. No branch can bear fruit by itself; it must remain in the vine."
JOHN 15:4 NIV

Each of us is connected to something or someone; some go so far as to say that we are all connected to each other in some way. We know what it's like to be affected by that connection in good ways and bad. Sometimes we find ourselves connected to people or things that aren't good for us or that prevent us from being the best person we can be. We need other people—but not so much when we are bound to the wrong person.

We can't go wrong when we live in unity with Christ. He is the "vine"—the life-giving force that will provide what we need to grow spiritually. As Christians, we were created to bear fruit, the fruit of the Spirit. Without our connection to Christ, our vine, our source of spiritual nutrition, we would wither and die. That connection is one of the greatest blessings of a life of faith in God.

What's Your Viewpoint?

We are hard pressed on every side, but not crushed; perplexed, but not in despair; persecuted, but not abandoned; struck down, but not destroyed.

2 Corinthians 4:8–9 niv

Perspective is a valuable tool. Without it, we turn minor events in our lives into larger-than-life calamities, immune to any intervention or solution. In the heat of the moment, we focus on the problem instead of the one who can solve it. But because of our relationship with Christ, we're never locked into a negative situation forever; He's always there with the key to free us from it.

No matter how bad things look or feel, our troubling circumstances are not permanent. We have hope in knowing nothing is too hard for God, and He wants nothing more than to reveal His power and give us His strength. When you feel buried under the weight of oppression, look up and see things from God's perspective. He always has the solution.

Words

The word of God is living and powerful, and sharper than any two-edged sword, piercing even to the division of soul and spirit, and of joints and marrow, and is a discerner of the thoughts and intents of the heart.

HEBREWS 4:12 NKJV

We have at our disposal the most powerful weapon in the universe against evil—the Bible. Yet we neglect to use it to its fullest potential. This weapon is multifaceted and easy to use. It never runs out of ammunition. We don't have to buy it, earn it, or ask for it, because we can hide its contents in our heart.

The Word of God is our gift from the Lord to assist, protect, heal, and instruct us, and to reveal who God is. It contains all the power we need. The wisdom it holds is there for us to absorb and apply to every situation. God has packed so much into His Word that it would take much longer than a lifetime to uncover all its mysteries.

It's All Good

Enter his gates with thanksgiving; go into his courts with praise. Give thanks to him and praise his name.

Psalm 100:4 NLT

Thankfulness is a mood lifter. Recognizing our blessings and humbling ourselves in gratitude can lift us above our feelings of hopelessness and despair. With our minds focused on the good things God has brought into our lives, we recognize negative things for what they are—intrusions designed to draw us away from God. We can choose to give thanks and see what God will do with it, or we can decide to stay stuck in our misery.

It is good to give praise to the God who created us—who gave us life and eternal security. When we honor Him with our thanks, He lets us share in the glory—and He sends even more blessings our way that we can be thankful for.

Forever with Jesus

We know that the one who raised the Lord Jesus
from the dead will also raise us with Jesus
and present us with you to himself.
2 CORINTHIANS 4:14 NIV

This earth is not our home. We must never become so attached to it that we forget the eternal dwelling place that is being prepared for us. Our thoughts must never get stuck in the perishable things of life; they need to be fixed on our eternal hope. How can we ever feel inconsolable if we have branded on our hearts the promise of eternity?

To be raised up means to be lifted to a higher position, to have increased worth. Only God can do this for us. He stands ready to promote us and bring us into His very presence. We can look forward to the day when His glorious face greets us in person.

Give and Receive

You will be enriched in every way so that you can be generous on every occasion, and through us your generosity will result in thanksgiving to God.

2 CORINTHIANS 9:11 NIV

The concept of generosity has taken quite a hit in our society. Selfless concern for the welfare of others is not a popular notion at a time when the economy has tanked and hardworking people are struggling to get by. And all too often, those who have more than enough to share—saints and sinners alike—treat with disdain and judgment the very people who need their help the most.

Have you ever felt the sting of poverty? If you have, you know how it feels to be treated so dismissively by people who cannot comprehend the difficulties you face. But God does. He nudges His people to provide for those who cannot provide for themselves. If you have an abundance, have you felt that nudge? God places a high value on generosity, much higher than we can imagine. Your generosity can start a whole new cycle of giving—and make all the difference in someone's life.

Deeper and Stronger

So then, just as you received Christ Jesus as Lord, continue to live your lives in him, rooted and built up in him, strengthened in the faith as you were taught, and overflowing with thankfulness.
Colossians 2:6–7 niv

Most people understand the principle of building on a firm foundation. We build our homes on deep footings so they will withstand just about anything that tries to tear them down—hurricanes, for instance. Even trees benefit from this principle; they become stronger and better able to stand against the wind when they send down deep roots to hold them steady.

When we apply that principle to faith, it's easy to see that the weaker our spiritual foundation—the closer to the surface our spiritual roots are—the more likely it is that the winds of deception will carry us away and cause our faith to collapse. But if we recognize God as our rock, our fortress, if we sink our roots way down deep and ground ourselves in His Word, we can withstand whatever comes against us. We don't ever have to be washed away by a storm.

Design for Holiness

Since God chose you to be the holy people he loves,
you must clothe yourselves with tenderhearted mercy,
kindness, humility, gentleness, and patience.
COLOSSIANS 3:12 NLT

God has chosen us for many things, but the highest calling we have is to holiness. This is also perhaps the hardest calling to fulfill. We certainly cannot do it in our own strength. The world is not attracted to our own righteousness; they see it for what it is—flawed. But they can detect truth in the reflection of God in us.

We have the opportunity to be clothed with the attributes of God. It's our responsibility to put on this godly attire every day. As we are getting dressed each morning, we can intentionally decide to wear His attributes so others can see those qualities that characterize God's holiness—and by extension, the qualities He graces us with as well.

Easy to Say

Don't worry about anything; instead, pray about everything. Tell God what you need, and thank him for all he has done.

PHILIPPIANS 4:6 NLT

Do you ever feel as if you spend too much time asking for things and not enough time giving thanks? We don't exactly live in a selfless world; we find ourselves constantly resisting all the dangling carrots of our society. But then our resistance comes up against the consumer philosophy of our day: We deserve to have anything and everything we want, because we're worth it. Instead of depending on God to meet our needs, we give in to that philosophy and indulge our wants.

When God does provide, we often forget to thank Him. We teach our little ones to say thank you, but we sometimes ignore that practice in our relationship with God. Why does God want us to have a thankful heart? It gives Him glory, and it gives us a healthy attitude—toward God and others who have blessed us.

Believe to Be Free

We live by believing and not by seeing.

2 Corinthians 5:7 NLT

For some, this scripture may be confusing, or even a bit intimidating. We naturally trust things we can see, touch, and recognize. We don't automatically put our trust in the invisible. But the visible things we trust are often what let us down.

To live life by believing in the unseen is a great test of our faith, and it is the great joy of our faith life. It puts control of the universe back into God's hands where it belongs. We don't have to shoulder the burden of making things happen. Through faith, we live free from the exhausting struggle to "see"—to see what's going on in someone's life, to see the results of our ministry to others, to see answers to our prayers. Faith in things you cannot see is believing God will do what He says He will do. That brings freedom.

Even in Your Weakness

We urge you, brothers and sisters, warn those who are idle and disruptive, encourage the disheartened, help the weak, be patient with everyone.

1 Thessalonians 5:14 NIV

This is a tall order for most of us who live busy lives. We're hard pressed to find time and emotional energy for ourselves and our families. How can we fulfill the requirements outlined here? Stress threatens to strangle us, and the demands of job, home, and church stretch us to our maximum output. Our fuse feels short. We withdraw because we can't give one more ounce of anything to anyone.

But this admonition is for everyone, and that means that when you feel you have nothing left to give, it's likely that a brother or sister in Christ will come along and begin serving you with God's love. Just as God sent you to others, He will send others to you.

Deeper Love Covers

Most important of all, continue to show deep love for each other, for love covers a multitude of sins.

1 Peter 4:8 NLT

If a friend was standing naked and alone in a crowd of accusers, would you stand by and do nothing, or would you rush to cover her with a blanket? This may seem like an overstatement of the sin problem, but really, it's an appropriate image. When our sins are exposed, we feel naked and judged. The first woman on this earth, Eve, experienced that shame. There was no friend there to cover her with love.

It's such a gift when someone steps up to help us, to mirror the Father's heart, especially when we've sinned. Instead of rejecting us, a true friend provides just what we need. This is love freely given, love that doesn't think about itself but gives of itself to us—no matter what we have done.

Smart Fruit

The wisdom that comes from heaven is first of all pure; then peace-loving, considerate, submissive, full of mercy and good fruit, impartial and sincere.
James 3:17 NIV

There are days when chaos seems to rule the house. No matter what you do, nothing works to slow things down or preserve sanity. You pull out every trick to help family members organize their schedules and tame bad attitudes. You thought you were smart enough to keep control. You thought you had enough knowledge to be authoritative. But the chaos continues.

Smarts and knowledge aren't enough to bear the fruit you and your family require to survive the hectic lifestyle that has become the norm for many of us. You need the wisdom that only comes from God to lift you above the chaos. Order is not out of your reach—it's yours for the asking.

We're Here for You

The human body has many parts, but the many parts make up one whole body. So it is with the body of Christ.

1 Corinthians 12:12 NLT

So many women have gone through times when they thought they could do it all. Like them, we take on more than we can handle and feel as if we are sinking. Sometimes pride is to blame, sometimes ignorance or unforeseen circumstances. Then when that immediate situation has passed, someone says to us, "Why didn't you ask for help? I would have been there for you."

We don't need to be alone when it comes to maneuvering through life's challenges. The Body of Christ is there to do its special part in any work God has asked us to do. Whether it's raising a family, starting a ministry, or building a program, we need to reach out to the whole body of helpers. God designed the Body of Christ in that way and for that purpose.

Perfected Love

We know how dearly God loves us, because he has given us the Holy Spirit to fill our hearts with his love.

Romans 5:5 NLT

God never leaves us hanging. He completes every plan, every design, every hope perfectly. There are no holes to fall into, no gaps to fill, and nothing left undone. That is how we know He works in us—He has perfected His love by giving us His Holy Spirit. There's no better proof of that than the fruit of His indwelling presence. We have the freedom to let Him use us for His purpose.

Having our hearts filled with the love of God is one of the results of that joyous union that keeps us close to Him and secure for eternity. We don't have to earn His love, He gives it freely. Once your heart belongs to Him, lesser kinds of love will never satisfy in quite the same way.

His Power in You

I did this so you would trust not in
human wisdom but in the power of God.
1 CORINTHIANS 2:5 NLT

It's wonderful to realize that we don't have to depend on the wisdom of humans, which is always imperfect. God's power plus our faith is a much more effective tool for survival than human wisdom will ever be. When our faith, no matter how small or large, teams up with the power that cannot be stopped, we are unstoppable. We can move forward with assurance that we will accomplish God's will in our family, our community, and our world.

Take your eyes off the intelligence of man and keep them fixed on the truth and might of God's Word and His Spirit in you. This is what will make the difference in your spiritual walk, the difference you have been longing for.

Fellowship to Encourage

When we get together, I want to encourage you in your faith, but I also want to be encouraged by yours.
ROMANS 1:12 NLT

The Body of Christ works best when we encourage one another in the faith and in life. Time spent with friends who share our beliefs gives us a chance to talk freely about Jesus and the wonderful things He has done for us. We can discover the blessing not only of being encouraged by a friend but also of encouraging that friend in return.

Christian fellowship provides a perfect opportunity to lift up the downtrodden, find solutions to life's problems, or offer a prayer of comfort. To varying degrees, God designed each of us to be a social creature. Someone out there can be a constant source of encouragement to you—and you can be the same to her.

Strength for Hard News

They will have no fear of bad news; their hearts are steadfast, trusting in the LORD.

PSALM 112:7 NIV

Waiting for your phone to ring—or vibrate—in the middle of a crisis can be grueling. Its silence convinces you that something horrible has happened and no one wants to call to give you the bad news. The anxiety you feel stems from the fear of the unknown. Questions run through your mind. Who will take care of this? What will happen to me? How bad will it get?

The only one who knows the answer to these questions is the one who holds the universe, and your life, in the palm of His hand. Recognizing His sovereignty in every situation can relieve you of the burden of worry. You don't have to let the fear of receiving bad news rob you of your peace. God is in control, and He has the answers to all of your questions. No news is so bad that He can't handle the crisis for you.

Don't Doubt

"What do you mean, 'If I can'?" Jesus asked.
"Anything is possible if a person believes."
MARK 9:23 NLT

Self-doubt will block the positive experiences we long to have, keeping us from seeing the miracles that encourage our faith to grow. We forget our position as a child of God. We neglect the power that is available to us when we are in the center of His will. We can do nothing in our own strength; we need to recognize that we can have confidence that the Holy Spirit will move mountains for us and provide us with infinite possibilities for our lives. The only limitation we have is that which we impose on ourselves by limiting our vision for what God will do for us.

God will help you in your unbelief. Ask Him to reveal all the possibilities for the situation you are in right now, the one that is troubling you. Our creative God knows how to make things happen.

You Will Understand

"I tell you the truth, if you had faith even as small as a mustard seed, you could say to this mountain, 'Move from here to there,' and it would move. Nothing would be impossible."

MATTHEW 17:20 NLT

Ever wonder why Jesus used the mustard seed as the example in this parable? Most of us think that it's because the mustard seed is the tiniest seed there is, and that is what makes His point relevant even to us today. However, the mustard seed isn't the smallest in the world—but that image was meaningful to the people He was speaking to.

The point of this parable is that we can do anything with our faith, even when our faith is small. The good news is so powerful that Jesus made sure those listening would understand that concept. Take time to listen to Jesus; His wisdom contains powerful truths.

Find Strength in Each Other

They strengthened the believers. They encouraged them to continue in the faith, reminding them that we must suffer many hardships to enter the Kingdom of God.

Acts 14:22 NLT

God has provided a kinship among believers for a purpose: He knows that serving Him can often take us down difficult roads. We face resistance and trouble, causing discouragement and doubt. We aren't always able to encourage ourselves and keep a sound perspective on the things that upset us. The Body of Christ works together for the kingdom.

A word of hope from a friend could make all the difference in building your faith. Strength for the next round of trouble can be found in others. When you open your heart to receive their help and make yourself available, God sends the right people your way.

Hope for Trust

I pray that God, the source of hope, will fill you completely with joy and peace because you trust in him. Then you will overflow with confident hope through the power of the Holy Spirit.

ROMANS 15:13 NLT

God does not ignore your faithfulness. Daily trust in Him opens the door to His blessings. With your heart prepared to receive, He pours joy and peace on you until you are overflowing with hope. This is important to your walk with Him. As you connect to the power it brings, boldness can be yours through the Holy Spirit.

God patiently waits for you to grow in confidence. The joy He gives is not like anything the world can give you. Trust is the key. Whether in big things or small, practice trusting God every day. The more you trust Him, the greater the likelihood you will experience the power you need for each day.

Honest Honor

"Yet a time is coming and has now come when the true worshipers will worship the Father in the Spirit and in truth, for they are the kind of worshipers the Father seeks."

John 4:23 niv

It's natural for us to gravitate toward people who appreciate us, largely because we crave validation. Sometimes, if we're especially needy of praise, we will put up with insincere individuals who compliment us out of selfish motives. Depending on our level of desperation, we may accept their false friendship, because it's better than none at all.

The Father doesn't need our praise and adoration, but worship is so engrained in the nature of fellowship that to neglect it is to miss out on one of the best aspects of our relationship with Him. God wants genuine fellowship with you. Open your heart and worship Him in Spirit and in truth.

Take the Cup

On the last and greatest day of the festival,
Jesus stood and said in a loud voice, "Let
anyone who is thirsty come to me and drink."
JOHN 7:37 NIV

There is a great incentive in finding water when you're dying of thirst; thirst, along with hunger, are the most powerful motivators in the human body. We need water even more than food to survive; the need for it is a powerful force that drives even the most stubborn person to find relief from dehydration.

We also experience a spiritual thirst we strive to satisfy. No ordinary waterhole will be sufficient to fill the emptiness inside. Only the water Jesus has to offer can satisfy that kind of thirst. He knows how much you need this living water. He doesn't want to see you suffer. He loves you so much that He holds out the cup, beckoning you to take it. Go ahead and drink!

Take Your Time

Let patience have its perfect work, that you may be perfect and complete, lacking nothing.

JAMES 1:4 NKJV

Can you imagine having everything you want in life? We are creatures of desire, and most of us never seem to be satisfied. Time moves too slowly. Our dreams take too long to be realized. We are willing to take shortcuts, to skip the proper order of things, to get what we want; patience doesn't come easily to our sinful nature.

But we miss so much when we rush to obtain those things we desire. God has a different way of dealing with our wants and our impatience: He teaches us endurance. We ask Him for something and the only answer we get from Him is "Wait." Learning this lesson may take considerable effort—but your journey toward maturity requires it.

Death to Life

Because of his great love for us, God, who is rich in mercy, made us alive with Christ even when we were dead in transgressions—it is by grace you have been saved.

Ephesians 2:4–5 niv

Among the different kinds of death we can experience is physical death, of course, but there are others as well—the death of a dream, for example. Spiritual death—the self-imposed separation of humanity from God—is a special kind of death: It can be reversed in an instant. Instead of being permanent, like physical death, the reality of spiritual death can turn on a dime. Turn to God in hope and humility, and He will immediately transform your spiritual death into a new—and much better—life. The lover of our souls works through His mercy and love to repair that which has caused us to be separated from Him.

We have been raised from the death we have chosen and brought back to the life with Christ we were meant to have. The gift of salvation is never dead. In truth, by His grace we receive new life each day.

How Great the Reward

Blessed is the one who perseveres under trial because, having stood the test, that person will receive the crown of life that the Lord has promised to those who love him.

James 1:12 NIV

Getting through a difficulty doesn't mean we have passed the test God intended for us to pass. There is a different kind of outcome and a special reward for those who persevered, those who persisted in faithfulness to the purpose of the trial. Perseverance is about being proactive rather than simply letting things happen and hoping you get by unharmed.

When we recognize there is purpose in our trials, we are able to praise God through them and anticipate a reward for our faithfulness. Having stayed the course despite the hardship, we receive the ultimate prize from God—the crown of life. That crown signifies that we are royalty in His eyes—children of the King.

Battles Already Won

Everyone born of God overcomes the world. This is the victory that has overcome the world, even our faith.
1 John 5:4 NIV

When it seems as if everything is against you and no one is on your side, victory looks too far away to be reached. The world looms so big sometimes that we sink into despair, losing bits of our faith by the minute. The turmoil around us mocks us and makes us feel small and unimportant.

We may live in the world, but we are not bound to its authority. Forces we can't see may push against us, but because we have the power of the Holy Spirit we can stand firm and resist the urge to give in. The victory is ours to win. Christ has already won the battle, and He lives in us, overcoming the forces that try to rob us of our faith. Don't worry; those forces will never win.

Enjoy the Light

Once you were full of darkness, but now you have light from the Lord. So live as people of light!

EPHESIANS 5:8 NLT

What is it about basking in the warm sun that elevates our mood? The gloomy days of winter have long since gone, and we are delighted to see bright days come. We seem to have more energy and enjoy being outside in the fresh air. The darkness has been lifted, and we are ready to move!

This is true when it comes to spiritual light as well. Our lives are more productive when we are out of the darkness, doing work for the kingdom of God. The difference is we don't have to wait for summer. God has delivered us from darkness into everlasting light. We can be free to live unencumbered by dark times—and spread the joy of His light in every season!

Dream Big

All glory to God, who is able, through his mighty power at work within us, to accomplish infinitely more than we might ask or think.

EPHESIANS 3:20 NLT

Do you dream big enough? Are your ambitions tied up with a nice red bow, sitting on a shelf in your mind? If you ask most women, they will tell you they have never realized their dreams. Most will say that it's too late or they have given up because of their circumstances. But giving up on your dreams isn't the plan God has for your life.

Maybe you are striving in your own power to make things happen. That's a common cause of unrealized dreams. It is through the power of Christ in us that we are able to continue on our journey toward fulfilling our dreams. He can accomplish so much more in us than our human minds can ever imagine. Dream big, think big—and ask for big miracles.

Tell It Like It Is

"They triumphed over him by the blood of the Lamb and by the word of their testimony; they did not love their lives so much as to shrink from death."

Revelation 12:11 NIV

Facts are not the same as truth. Our interpretation of what we see and hear is not reliable. Yet we look at facts and trust our eyes and ears, and determine that this is what we should trust when deciding how we should live. Is it no wonder victory over evil is not ours? But it can be!

Victory in the battles in your life has already been won through the blood of Jesus. When you proclaim the truth, nothing can stand against you. But remember—this is not the truth as the world sees it, but it is the truth spoken to you through the presence of Jesus in your heart and mind. What a joy to know that we have God's truth on our side!

The Shield of Faith

Take up the shield of faith, with which you can extinguish all the flaming arrows of the evil one.
Ephesians 6:16 NIV

Those burning arrows! Some days it seems as if we are pulling them out by the hour. On those days when we aren't feeling well, battling fatigue or confusion, it's impossible to thwart the enemy on our own. Our faith is weak, and defeat is looming on the horizon.

But we have a shield to protect us. Our faith, no matter how small, is able to stop the burning pain of attack by evil forces. Just by holding our faith up to Satan, we can challenge his authority over us. The call to carry faith with us as a weapon works to our benefit; God provides the tools for victory even when we feel helpless.

Proclaim It!

We are Christ's ambassadors; God is making his appeal through us. We speak for Christ when we plead, "Come back to God!"
2 Corinthians 5:20 NLT

For most of us, fear grips our hearts when we think of pleading a case in front of a cloud of witnesses. We may have written our speech and practiced our vocal projection. We may have important things to say and may want very much to be heard. After all, we speak for God.

Yet, there is the terror, holding us back.

If we speak for God, He will have our back. The outcome is not our responsibility; the work is His. His message needs a mouthpiece, and we are chosen to be the instrument to deliver it. He gives us the words and the power to stand behind them. Remember how blessed you were when someone proclaimed the good news to you? Now it's your turn to bless someone else by returning the favor.

The Tallest Peak Is Yours

In your strength I can crush an army;
with my God I can scale any wall.
PSALM 18:29 NLT

We look up at a high mountain and wonder how any person could scale it. The enormity of it sends chills up our back, and we feel small in its shadow. Surely God would never ask us to climb such a dangerous peak, would He? But He knows we can do it with His help; to Him the mountain is not so big and terrifying.

In our hurry to live life, we forget to tone our faith muscles with the strength of God. Scaling mountains is good practice for endurance when the really tough battles come. And God stands at the top, holding you with a tether so strong it cannot be broken. He gently guides you, telling you where to place your foot. Look up—He's got you in His strong arms, and He will never let you go.

You Were Chosen

"You did not choose me, but I chose you and appointed you so that you might go and bear fruit—fruit that will last—and so that whatever you ask in my name the Father will give you."

JOHN 15:16 NIV

Remember when your favorite grade school teacher chose you out of all the other kids to do a special job? She made you feel as if you were the best child for the assignment. You felt such pride and wanted more than anything to do a good job for her. When she praised you, you thought you could accomplish anything.

The Father didn't wait for you to choose Him. He scooped you up and called you His own, appointing you to a special task. Receiving His life means you will bear the kind of fruit He rewards. In His name, you are able to gather up all the gifts He has in store for you.

Spiritual Weapons

We are human, but we don't wage war as humans do. We use God's mighty weapons, not worldly weapons, to knock down the strongholds of human reasoning and to destroy false arguments.

2 Corinthians 10:3–4 NLT

Humans can be persuasive people. The right argument, expressed by just the right person in just the right way, can sway us from our most solid opinions. Debating an issue with an effective wordsmith can erode our confidence and water down our convictions. At times, we may even be convinced of principles that are contrary to God's Word.

We always have God's truth to stand on, however. No human reasoning can change a word of it. When we take time to engrain it into our minds, asking the Holy Spirit to brand us with it, we are able to hold fast to our beliefs—and with boldness demolish the arguments of those who oppose God.

Be Aware

"The thief comes only to steal and kill and destroy; I have come that they may have life, and have it to the full."
JOHN 10:10 NIV

We don't need to live life watching for a boogeyman around every corner. But God wants us to be aware that there are dangers lurking in this world. Evil forces want to bring us down and steer us away from God. When we aren't on our guard, we can be vulnerable to their cunning devices.

God wants us to pay attention to the death traps of the world. Jesus came to earth and sacrificed His life so that we may live abundant life even in the midst of danger. His great love for us demands that His protective hand be upon us at all times. We may come close to the traps set for us, but we can be confident of His constant protection.

What Is Best

O Lord my God, I cried to you for help,
and you restored my health.
Psalm 30:2 NLT

God never promised that life would be perfect. We live in a world of sickness and disease, the realities of which we cannot deny or avoid altogether. Healing from God sometimes comes instantaneously and sometimes takes a lifetime. Only He is in control of life and death.

But we can be sure that He wants what is best for us, no matter what our disposition. He looks on the whole person, spiritually and physically. We cannot see the future or pretend to guess what the outcome of our lives will be—with one exception. We do know that abundant life is not dependent on our physical state.

When we cry out to God in our times of physical need, He may answer in a way we don't understand—but He always knows and does what is right for us.

Forget It

"I will forgive their wickedness and will remember their sins no more."

HEBREWS 8:12 NIV

As overworked and multitasking women, it's not unusual for us to forget things now and then. Our busy schedules and constant juggling of family activities can block our ability to remember everything and keep everyone's lives on track. But there is one thing we are not likely to ever forget—the offense or betrayal we have felt from a friend. The sting seems to last forever.

Our example for forgetting wrongs is the God of forgiveness. He has not only forgiven our sins, but He has also removed them from His memory and removed them from the account of our debt. When we learn to practice intentional forgetfulness—the kind that purposely forgets the wrongs done to us—we will be free to love and fellowship with others in the way God intended.

Like New

"I restore the crushed spirit of the humble and revive the courage of those with repentant hearts."

ISAIAH 57:15 NLT

Have you ever seen a dilapidated and blemished piece of furniture that has been restored to its original beauty? The grain of the wood and character of its style are reborn to look new and usable again. What about that plant you neglected and now looks as if it will die? It has withered beyond any hope of you reviving it, and you've considered throwing it away. But then a friend with a green thumb rescues it and restores it to new life.

Thanks be to God that He rescues us from the trash heaps and garbage cans of the world! Is your spirit crushed? Has every bit of courage been sucked out of you? He'll restore you and revive all that is broken in your life—just surrender your blemished life, give Him your heart, and let Him make you shiny and new again.

God's Army

The Lord told Gideon, "With these 300 men I will rescue you and give you victory over the Midianites. Send all the others home."

Judges 7:7 NLT

We spend too much time building an army for the battles in our lives. We try to determine how much firepower we need to obtain victory. We have strategies to develop, weapons to form, and warriors to assemble. But in our frenzy to prepare for battle, we have forgotten who has the real power to win the war.

God instructed Gideon to pare down his army from tens of thousands to three hundred. Imagine the initial fear in Gideon's heart when he realized he would be going into battle with so few men. But the wonderful lesson for Gideon, and for us, is that when God chooses the warriors, they'll be sufficient to win the battle. Don't get caught up in numbers. You only need one warrior fighting for you.

Lean In

We know and rely on the love God has for us. God is love.
Whoever lives in love lives in God, and God in them.
1 John 4:16 niv

There are days, weeks, and sometimes years when we feel we have nothing to stand on. Life's chaos and pain drag time out by the hours, and we wonder what we can grab onto in order to steady ourselves. Encouragement seems a distant friend instead of a constant companion. We search the horizon for some stability.

What can we rely on? The love of God. When all else fails, crumbles, or drains our strength, we always have His abiding love to lean on. We cohabitate with God in His love and wave it as a flag to anyone who needs His love to get through their long day. His love steadies us and keeps us from falling.

Submit and Surrender

Submit yourselves, then, to God.
Resist the devil, and he will flee from you.
JAMES 4:7 NIV

Submission is an act of the will, but it also involves the surrender of our hearts. In contrast to what that implies, we actually gain strength in giving up our own will to accept the power of God instead. This is the key to resisting evil—the power of God in us. We aren't swatting a fly; we are battling an evil force, and we need that kind of power.

The great promise is that if in God's power we repel the attempts of evil to trip us up, he'll turn tail and run. He wants no part of God's redemptive work. He will flee, but he will come back another day to try again. But if you are in submission and fully surrendered to God, you have the power to reject him every time he tries to bother you.

Always the Same

Every good and perfect gift is from above,
coming down from the Father of the heavenly lights,
who does not change like shifting shadows.
James 1:17 NIV

People change. Relationships take hits and may die when things change too quickly or drastically. People make and break promises, and at times it seems we can count on no one—not even ourselves! Even those who once encouraged us in our talents and gifts may give up on us when we need them the most.

The lights in the heavens and the solid earth under our feet may shift, but the Creator of all will not change. He will never stop giving gifts and blessings, because it is His very nature to give to us generously. He wants to pour good things into your life. You can be assured of one thing that will never change—God won't change His mind about you!

Shun the Dark

If we walk in the light as He is in the light,
we have fellowship with one another, and the blood
of Jesus Christ His Son cleanses us from all sin.
1 John 1:7 NKJV

As long as we stay in the dark, we are able to hide who we really are, as well as all our secrets. In the dark, our imperfections go unnoticed—as do our good qualities and gifts. Genuine fellowship must take place in the light so we can see each other's faces and personalities. Being with others reveals a lot about ourselves. Sharing our victories with others confirms that God is at work in our lives.

God has provided the light for you! You don't have to hide in the dark, afraid that you may be the only one who has sinned. There are others who need you to come out of your hiding and into the light of salvation in Jesus.

Fire Up!

This is why I remind you to fan into flames the spiritual gift God gave you when I laid my hands on you.

2 TIMOTHY 1:6 NLT

It's hard to fan the flame when you feel you don't have a spark to start with. Circumstances and bad news may have doused your embers, and you don't know if you can get them fired up again. Neither do you know what to fan them with, and even if you did know, you wonder if you have the strength to make it happen.

But those gifts, once they're flaming again, will give you the fire you need to do the work you must do. The gifts are not just for the sake of others; they also serve a purpose with regard to your spiritual health. When you are exercising your God-given gifts, you find the spiritual energy to keep going even when life tries to beat you down.

Look Forward to Glory

Because of our faith, Christ has brought us into this place of undeserved privilege where we now stand, and we confidently and joyfully look forward to sharing God's glory.

Romans 5:2 NLT

Just when we think we have lost the battle, when our defenses are down and we have no hope of living through the war for our souls, God places us in a position of safety. He extends to us the gift of solid ground, and once again we feel confident and able to release our fear to receive joy. We can see beyond the trouble of the day and know without a doubt that God will let us participate in the glory of victory.

This is our great motivation to keep working on building up our faith. It affords us privilege, joy, confidence, and shared glory—enough to last us an eternity!

Forever Rejoicing

Always be full of joy in the Lord. I say it again—rejoice!
PHILIPPIANS 4:4 NLT

This short statement of encouragement is more than it appears to be. There is a hint of a command, an exhortation, and maybe also a warning. God always deserves our praise and rejoicing. Given all that He has done for us, we could rejoice forever and never cover all of His great blessings. But rejoicing does some good things for us too. It pumps up our faith and reminds us of the many things we have to be thankful for. We are also reminded that the potential for trouble is always around the corner and that rejoicing will help us take hold of the power that lifts us up and helps us persevere.

What have we to lose by rejoicing? Nothing. We need to pull it up from deep within us and experience the joy it brings, day by day.

Complete Circle

"Until now you have not asked for anything in my name. Ask and you will receive, and your joy will be complete."

JOHN 16:24 NIV

God longs to give you the desires of your heart. Asking in the name of Jesus puts us in line with His will for what our wants should be and what our needs really are. As we take on the mind of Christ, the more likely we are to want the best things, the right things. This is what ultimately brings the joy—knowing we are one with Christ in our desires.

We can be confident in knowing we have just what we need when we have asked and received what His will for us is. Confidence brings joy, and receiving what truly fulfills our longings brings us full circle. We are complete and satisfied when we ask and receive in gratitude, praising Him for our joy.

Rejoice in the Unity

I delight greatly in the LORD; my soul rejoices in my God.
For he has clothed me with garments of salvation
and arrayed me in a robe of his righteousness.
ISAIAH 61:10 NIV

Like a bride anticipating her wedding day, so God's children anticipate the day when He brings them to Himself. And just as the bride experiences the joy of her wedding day, so we experience the joy and thanksgiving of knowing what it's like to belong to Him. He prepares the celebration and clothes us with His righteousness.

We have won the heart of our groom. He welcomes us into His family. We can see how much He has done for us and plans to do in the future. We are a bride of the King!

Rejoice in knowing He chose you to receive salvation. It's your day—but it's one that never ends.

Holy Trust

Our heart shall rejoice in Him, because
we have trusted in His holy name.
PSALM 33:21 NKJV

As children we learn to put our trust in many things, some of which are not trustworthy at all; we're much too young to make wise decisions all the time. In most cases, we first place our trust in our parents, and then we begin to trust other close relatives. As teens, we find out that trusting the wrong person can be hurtful and even disastrous. Lessons about trust can be hard ones to learn, and sometimes we carry the consequences of poor choices for the rest of our lives.

What a relief it is to finally discover that there is actually a God we can trust with our whole being. He cannot fail us, because He is infallible. He will not forsake us, because He is holy. We can take Him at His word in every situation. That's the kind of trust we can build our lives on.

Choose the True Light

"Put your trust in the light while there is still time; then you will become children of the light."

John 12:36 NLT

Are you sitting in the living room of your spiritual life with every lamp turned on, trying to illuminate your path? It's not perfect light, but it reveals most of what you need to know. You can make your choices based on lamplight and probably get by. You can hope the current doesn't fail and you won't be left in the dark again.

Instead, why not turn off the artificial light and open wide the windows to let the real light of the Son come in? His illumination is brighter than all those lamps, and His is the only light that can heal you and dispel evil.

Let Jesus be your permanent light source. There's no better kind of illumination.

Eyes on Jesus

My eyes are always on the Lord, for he rescues me from the traps of my enemies.

Psalm 25:15 NLT

When our focus strays from Jesus, we go our own way, falling into snares that we didn't know were there. When we are sidetracked by distractions, we veer off and run the risk of becoming lost and surrounded by hidden traps. He wants to show us the safe path, the one that goes around the enemy of our soul, He walks ahead of us, looking back to see if we are following His lead.

Jesus never leaves us behind. He hears our cries for help, and He comes to our aid. You can try to rush ahead of Him, but He is never behind you—He is always in front, removing the snares from your path.

Thanks to Jesus, we don't have to walk blindly into danger. He is always there to safely guide us.

Right and Power

To all who believed him and accepted him,
he gave the right to become children of God.
John 1:12 NLT

To be given a right is to be given power. As children of God, we have been given the influence and authority that comes with our position in the family. Once you are part of a family, you have much more than just a name. Think of being a child of God in terms of being given a position of liberty and strength. We are not merely heirs; we actually participate in the Father's activities.

This is a new way to view ourselves. We are not just God's daughters; we are also His representatives, just as if we were representing a family name. A great responsibility? Yes. A great honor? Yes. We now have a place where we belong, a place saved for us by a loving God.

Unbound

Christ is the culmination of the law so that there may be righteousness for everyone who believes.

ROMANS 10:4 NIV

If you have ever seen a show in which a character has been tied up or bound in chains, you have seen what it's like to be in bondage. We don't have to be physically constrained to feel restricted and fear retaliation for any misstep we make. There are rules of man and rules of God. Christ came to abolish the law that kept us tied up with sin and condemnation. We have access to the mercy and grace of God that unties our bindings and instructs us not through a written law but through the spirit of the law impressed on our hearts.

God wants you to live free. Jesus died so you could break away from the righteous laws of man and have communion with Him by His Spirit living in you. Never forget that you are free!

He's Calling You

"Do not fear, for I have redeemed you;
I have summoned you by name; you are mine."
ISAIAH 43:1 NIV

There is something about being called by name that warms our heart. Some businesses advise employees to ask for their customers' names and use it in conversation. It puts you at ease to think that a person cares enough to know your name. Even though you know they may not be sincere, you still like the bit of familiarity.

We know for certain that when God calls our name, He knows whom He is calling. He knows your name, and He knows your true self. You are His child, and He has watched you from before you were born, always wanting the best for you. He knows when you are in danger and calls to you to warn you. Just hearing His voice is enough to calm your fears. Make sure you listen for His call.

Too Big?

"When you pass through the waters, I will be with you; and when you pass through the rivers, they will not sweep over you. When you walk through the fire, you will not be burned."

Isaiah 43:2 niv

Deep waters, overwhelming troubles, trials by fire, and hard times don't faze the Father. He doesn't tremble at the calamities that befall you. He isn't worried that circumstances are too big for you or for Him. He isn't wringing His hands, wondering how things will turn out. He already has it covered.

We look at our problems and panic at the sight of them. We leap before we look; we recoil before we reach up to grab the hand of God. He rescues us, although not always in the way or in the timing we think He should. We need to understand and believe that He has our problems under His control. The God who created the universe and everything in it cannot be overwhelmed by anything—especially our problems.

He's There to Help You

"I am the Lord your God who takes hold of your right hand and says to you, Do not fear; I will help you."
Isaiah 41:13 NIV

When we cross streams that are swift and rocky, we fear we could slip any minute. The current pushes us one way, and we wobble trying to keep ourselves upright. The shore seems so far away, and yet it's too late to go back. Without a sure footing, we are afraid to move at all. How will we make it to safety?

It only takes a firm outstretched hand or a tight and secure rope to make us feel safe again. God is at your side, holding out His hand to steady you. When we take our eyes off the raging water and turn to hear Him speak, He will take our hand and lead us safely home.

Trust at All Times

Trust in Him at all times, you people; pour out your heart before Him; God is a refuge for us.

PSALM 62:8 NKJV

How often have God's people cried out to Him in despair? The downtrodden, the desperate, and the hurting pour out their pain to the Father and learn that trusting Him opens doors to places of refuge and shoulders to cry on. What more could we ask?

The call to trust God isn't just for the hard times. We also need to be totally dependent on Him in the times when we feel confident and content. The hidden twists of life sneak up behind us when our guard is down and we are floating on the breeze of complacency. Our independent nature is meaningless and even counterproductive in the presence of God. It's when we lean on Him that we are the strongest.

No Place Like Home

"My Father's house has many rooms; if that were not so, would I have told you that I am going there to prepare a place for you?"
John 14:2 NIV

What child doesn't want their own room? A place to be by yourself, have friends over, or have that special feeling of possession. If you were fortunate, you had a place where you could go that was all yours. You could be in your parents' house but still have your personal domain.

Our Father has not only invited you to His house, but He has also prepared a special room for you. It's a better place than you've ever been, and He has your heart in mind as He gets your place ready for you. Are you ready to receive? Are you ready to step across the threshold? You can start getting excited about your eternal home even now!

Pain's Demise

"He will wipe every tear from their eyes,
and there will be no more death or sorrow or
crying or pain. All these things are gone forever."
REVELATION 21:4 NLT

God knows you're frustrated with the sadness of life. Sometimes it seems the trials will never end. You wish you could reach the bottom of the pit so that the only place left to go was up—or better yet, escape the pain altogether.

We question why we have to experience pain and death and sorrow. We cry out to God and ask, "How long, O Lord?"

In heaven we will no longer be bound by the physical laws of earth. Living without pain and tears is hard to fathom. But this is the promise of heaven for eternity. Death cannot remain in the house of the one who conquered it for you.

There's Still Time

Jesus answered him, "Truly I tell you,
today you will be with me in paradise."
LUKE 23:43 NIV

Imagine the relief felt by the thief who hung on the cross next to Jesus. Surely he was stunned to hear that his eternity had been salvaged. After all he had done, he knew he didn't deserve to be pardoned. But Jesus had mercy on him, even as he hung there in agony and shame. It was an unlikely place to be offered forgiveness of sin.

Or was it?

Jesus meets us where we are and extends His hand of mercy and grace to everyone. Could this be any better proof of His desire to forgive? In His very worst hour, Jesus reached out to a sinner who had no chance to redeem himself. How blessed we are to have the assurance that our eternity has been salvaged as well!

His Greatness

Since ancient times no one has heard, no ear has perceived, no eye has seen any God besides you, who acts on behalf of those who wait for him.

Isaiah 64:4 niv

If you've ever visited the great cathedrals of the world, you can see by the magnificent architecture and masterful artwork that the people worshiped a God who was worthy of all honor and glory. Theirs was a big God, and they committed a lifetime of backbreaking work and sacrifice to build a temple for Him that many would not live to see completed. To stand inside these magnificent cathedrals is a humbling experience.

The world's view of God's grandeur has changed considerably since medieval times, when so many stunning cathedrals were built. Ours is a not-so-big God to a world that considers Him ineffectual and irrelevant. But we know better, and because we do, we need to give Him the honor that is due Him. He is deserving of the most impressive cathedral on earth and so much more. He is deserving of everything we have to give.

His Lost Sheep

"Do not be afraid, little flock, for your Father has been pleased to give you the kingdom."

LUKE 12:32 NIV

Sheep are by nature followers. They follow the shepherd to find food and shelter, and the shepherd leads them away from danger to a place of protection that he has prepared for them. The shepherd knows the value of his flock; he knows that they may wander off, and he may have to retrieve them. He knows they would be lost without him.

Our Father tenderly and patiently shepherds us for the purpose of guiding us to the safety of heaven. He knows we are afraid of the dangers out there, and comforts us even when we have wandered off on our own way. He brings us home every time—and He promises us the kingdom.

Your House

We know that if our earthly house, this tent,
is destroyed, we have a building from God, a house
not made with hands, eternal in the heavens.
2 CORINTHIANS 5:1 NKJV

Most people take pride in their homes. They work hard to make them comfortable and attractive. Some people go to great lengths and expense to outdo the rest of the neighborhood, especially when it comes to outdoor Christmas displays. In many cities are great mansions and towering monuments to the finest styles of architecture.

All of this is temporal and could disappear in an instant. Fire, flood, or earthquake can turn our earthly homes, no matter how spectacular, into piles of useless rubble. Not so with our eternal home, which will be beautiful and magnificently lit with the light of heaven. And it will be all ours, custom-built just for us.

Perfect Road Maps

"I know the plans I have for you," declares the *Lord, "plans to prosper you and not to harm you, plans to give you hope and a future."*
JEREMIAH 29:11 NIV

Many women want to follow a plan. Whether it's a plan for the day or the week—for dinner tomorrow, appointments for the kids, or a road trip agenda—Mom usually has to make sure potential disaster is averted by keeping a schedule of some sort. We lean heavily on our plans, and when they get turned upside down, so do we.

If only we could see into the future as God does, we'd know what to expect at every moment. But that also means that we would never face the obstacles that we need to overcome in order to be spiritually mature. A plan without roadblocks sounds delightful, but it's through faith during challenging times that we learn and grow and please God. Let Him make your plans today.

The Blessed Circle

No matter how many promises God has made,
they are "Yes" in Christ. And so through him the
"Amen" is spoken by us to the glory of God.
2 Corinthians 1:20 niv

We are partakers in God's glory, whether it's in the big miracles that change the course of our lives or the little blessings that touch our family life during the day. At times it is incomprehensible that our seemingly insignificant lives are tied to the will of the Father. But it all starts with Him.

God includes us in the circle of His will, and we are blessed each time we reach out and touch the truth of His Word for us—the truth that gives us hope and significance, which are only available in Him.

God's Perfect Order

If we confess our sins, he is faithful and just and will forgive us our sins and purify us from all unrighteousness.

1 John 1:9 NIV

We depend on recipes to give us the right directions for preparing new and unfamiliar dishes. When an ingredient is missing from a recipe, the end result suffers; the dish is not at all what we anticipated. In a sense, God has given us a "recipe" for accessing His forgiveness, but this recipe lists only one ingredient: confession. Leave that out, and we can never experience complete forgiveness and purification.

God is the God of order. Not only did He create orderly systems, He also developed procedures that make them work. The procedure for making the forgiveness and purification system work depends on our willingness to acknowledge the sin in our lives. Once we do that, we can be assured that we will have what we anticipated—the grace to move beyond our sin and enjoy the fresh start that God has given us.

Expecting Too Much

Make allowance for each other's faults,
and forgive anyone who offends you. Remember,
the Lord forgave you, so you must forgive others.
COLOSSIANS 3:13 NLT

Expectations can be a dangerous thing. We usually have the wrong ones for the wrong people. We set man-made rules and guidelines and try to make them fit every personality and every situation. This often causes pain for both the one who is burdened by unrealistic expectations and the one who imposes them.

Have you felt the weight of improbable expectations—maybe someone's belief that you should be perfect in every way? Be encouraged; Jesus sees your individuality, and more than anyone else, He knows you're not perfect. He knows every one of your faults; He has seen every one of your offenses against someone else. And He has forgiven all of it. The best thing you can do in return is this: Go and do likewise.

Our Dream Gift

The wages of sin is death, but the gift of God is eternal life in Christ Jesus our Lord.
ROMANS 6:23 NKJV

As children we dream of the gifts we want, never understanding that we won't get them all. And we really don't believe that if we misbehave, they may be taken away from us as punishment. We're at the mercy of our parents to decide if and when we should get them back. Most of us cannot help but dream about whatever we think will bring us happiness. We think about it every day—sometimes all day! Yet we know our sin keeps us from the full reward—the gifts we so desperately want.

But we have been promised a gift that will secure all the dreams of our soul. Other gifts pale in comparison. Eternal life is ours—because we abide in Christ.

Watchful Waiting

Devote yourselves to prayer, being watchful and thankful.

Colossians 4:2 NIV

How many times have you heard someone testify that after years of praying for something, what they wanted came to pass? Persistence seems to have been the key, but everyone who's been in this situation likely had periods of doubt. And then when the answer comes, we may be surprised; we are caught with our faith weak and small. Still, God was faithful to bring about the answer; despite being caught off guard, we can give Him praise and thanks.

How much more encouraged we will be when we see the answer coming and participate in the excitement. This can only happen if we stay in tune with what God is saying and remain alert as if we were waiting for a special event. If we pray, believe, and look for the answer, we can also praise God for letting us participate in bringing the answer to pass.

He Is Near

The Lord is close to all who call on him,
yes, to all who call on him in truth.
Psalm 145:18 NLT

Sometimes when we call on God, He seems to be silent. We fret and complain, thinking He has let us down, and we return to our hit-or-miss faith. Had we kept the ultimate truth of God's faithfulness hidden in our hearts and foremost in our minds, we might not have felt that there was any distance at all between God and our hopes and dreams.

God's truth is what anchors your faith; your faith is what gets His attention. The truth is readily available to you. He wants you to know He is nearby. He waits for you to grasp all that He has for you—and reap the blessings that come your way when you embrace a relationship with Him that is founded on trust.

Keep Knocking

"Ask and it will be given to you; seek and you will find; knock and the door will be opened to you. For everyone who asks receives; the one who seeks finds; and to the one who knocks, the door will be opened."
MATTHEW 7:7–8 NIV

If you've ever tried your hand at door-to-door sales—maybe as a teenager selling magazines to raise funds for your school—you know the anxiety you felt as you waited for the door to open. You didn't know what to expect, even if you knew some of your potential customers. Would the person behind the door greet you with a smile and give you a huge order? Or would they scowl and slam the door in your face before you finished your carefully practiced sales pitch?

God promises us that if we ever come to His door and knock, He will open the door and give us what we ask for. We don't even need a sales pitch; a simple request will do. Imagine how different your fundraising venture would have gone had that been the case! Now imagine how you would feel if someone made that promise to you today. Well, someone has—and He's waiting to hear your knock at His door.

Strength for Weakness

He gives strength to the weary and
increases the power of the weak.
ISAIAH 40:29 NIV

No one likes to feel weak and powerless. We certainly appreciate those times when we are at the top of our game, with strength to spare. But often it seems as if our lack of strength rolls from one day to the next with no end in sight. We tried to do it all, and now we are suffering. We have nothing left with which to make it through a single day.

The good news is that we have an endless supply of strength in God. He is the ultimate source of energy in our lives. He sees what we need to do each day, and He gives us the strength to accomplish those things. When our energy runs out, we can be fairly certain that either we're doing more than we should or we need to stop relying on our own strength—and start drawing on the power God has given us.

With You All the Time

"The LORD your God is living among you. He is a mighty savior. He will take delight in you with gladness. With his love, he will calm all your fears. He will rejoice over you with joyful songs."

ZEPHANIAH 3:17 NLT

Do any of us ever fully appreciate all that God does for us? Can we? Probably not, because we can't even see most of what He does. But think about just these few actions on our behalf: He lives among us so we need never be alone. Just when we need to be rescued, He saves us. He even delights in us—we who rejected Him! When fear paralyzes us, God calms us and gets us moving again. He rejoices over us, singing the songs of heaven.

Does this sound like the God you know? If not, why not? Neither His character nor His truth has changed. Right this minute, He is blessing you with His love and care, fighting your battles, and encouraging you in your victories. We'll never see all that He does, but when we truly open our eyes, we can see more—much more.

Mark Your Calendar

In their hearts humans plan their course,
but the LORD establishes their steps.
PROVERBS 16:9 NIV

Are you a list maker? Do you depend on your calendar to get through each day, organizing your family's schedule so nothing falls through the cracks? If so, you likely consider planning to be a chore worth doing so your household can function with as few mishaps as possible.

But what about the Lord's plans for us? How do they fit into our carefully planned lives? Even if we have sought His will in every matter, we need to be flexible and leave room for Him to surprise us with a major shift in our plans. In doing so, He reminds us that He is in control, and nothing we enter on our calendars can be considered permanent. When we surrender to this truth, we can turn on a dime and follow Him in a new direction, knowing that the outcome will be for our good. He always has our best interests at heart.

He Was and Is

To us a child is born, to us a son is given,
and the government will be on his shoulders.
And he will be called Wonderful Counselor,
Mighty God, Everlasting Father, Prince of Peace.
Isaiah 9:6 NIV

Jesus started His earthly life as an innocent baby in a manger. He later became a defiant boy who had the audacity to speak to adults in the temple. Later still, He was a carpenter at His father's side. And then, He began His very own ministry after calling twelve ordinary men to join Him as He proclaimed the kingdom of God. Jesus calmed the seas, healed the sick, and turned water into wine.

Now He, our risen Lord, is sitting at the right hand of our Father, waiting for us to join Him for eternity. His earthly life has come and gone, but He has always been and will always be the Wonderful Counselor, Mighty God, Everlasting Father, the Prince of Peace. Imagine: He is all that and more, and yet He knows your name!

Peace to You

May the Lord of peace himself give you peace at all times and in every way. The Lord be with all of you.
2 THESSALONIANS 3:16 NIV

People for peace—not only the absence of strife but also the deep comfort and serenity of knowing that all will be well. We see glimpses of it, but we are too busy to stop and let it fall on us and permeate our lives. We pray for it, but all too often we run when God offers it to us. We're afraid we'll be disappointed; not even God's peace can last very long, right?

Our distrust of God is the problem. We can't understand His peace if we've never experienced it, but if we would trust Him, we could know what it feels like to bask in the calming, healing peace of the Father. The next time you catch a glimpse of it, stop what you're doing and immerse yourself in His peace. It's available to you at all times and in every way.

Scripture Index

OLD TESTAMENT

Isaiah

Jeremiah

Lamentations

Nahum

Zephaniah

NEW TESTAMENT

Matthew

Mark

Luke

John